DIGITAL ACCESSIBILITY
THE ENTERPRISE JOURNEY

DIGITAL ACCESSIBILITY
THE ENTERPRISE JOURNEY

BY

CHLOE ROBINSON
DARYLLYN BROOKS

KNOWLEDGE

KNOWLEDGE BAKERS

ISBN: 9789390013265 (HB)

Published by : **Knowledge Bakers**
Pune, India
Email: knowledgebakers2019@gmail.com

PREFACE

Digital accessibility refers to the practice of designing digital content and technology that can be accessed and used by all people, including those with disabilities. With the increasing importance of digital content in our daily lives, digital accessibility has become a critical issue for businesses and organizations worldwide. There are many types of disabilities that can affect how people interact with digital content, including visual, hearing, motor, and cognitive disabilities. For example, people with visual disabilities may use screen readers to access digital content, while people with hearing disabilities may rely on captions or transcripts to understand audio content.

Digital accessibility is essential for many reasons. Firstly, it is a matter of social justice and human rights. Access to digital content and technology is increasingly important for many aspects of life, such as education, employment, and social interactions. Therefore, it is critical that everyone, regardless of their abilities, can access and use digital content. Secondly, digital accessibility is also a matter of legal compliance. Many countries have laws and regulations that require businesses and organizations to provide digital content that is accessible to people with disabilities. Failure to comply with these laws can result in legal consequences, including fines and lawsuits. Thirdly, digital accessibility is also good for business. By designing digital content that is accessible to everyone, businesses can expand their customer base, increase user engagement and loyalty, and improve their reputation. It can also help businesses avoid the costs associated with legal challenges and redesigning inaccessible digital content.

To achieve digital accessibility, there are several key principles that businesses and organizations should follow. These include using accessible technologies, providing alternative formats, such as captions and transcripts, designing content for flexibility, and ensuring compatibility with assistive technologies, such as screen readers and voice recognition software. There are also several guidelines and standards that businesses can follow to ensure digital accessibility. The Web Content Accessibility Guidelines (WCAG), developed by the World Wide Web Consortium (W3C), are the most widely recognized guidelines for digital accessibility. The guidelines provide a set of recommendations for making digital content more accessible to people with disabilities. By following principles and guidelines for digital accessibility, businesses and organizations can ensure that their digital content is accessible to everyone, regardless of their abilities. This can help to create a more inclusive and accessible digital environment for everyone.

This book provides a practical guide to implementing digital accessibility within an enterprise, covering everything from creating a culture of accessibility to hiring staff and developing procurement policies that prioritize accessibility. Provides a comprehensive overview of digital accessibility, its importance, and its impact on businesses and also focuses on the role of a committee or team responsible for ensuring digital accessibility within an enterprise. Describes how to create a culture of digital accessibility within an enterprise, including how to raise awareness among employees and foster a commitment to accessibility throughout the organization. Focuses on how to develop procurement policies that prioritize accessibility when purchasing technology, software, or services. It may also discuss how to create an accessibility policy that outlines an enterprise's commitment to accessibility.

We are grateful to all those persons as well as various books, manuals, periodicals, magazines, journals etc. that helped in the preparation of this book. In spite of the best efforts, it is possible that some errors may have occurred into the compilation and editing of the book. Further queries, constructive suggestions and criticisms for the improvement of the book are always welcomed and shall be thankfully acknowledged.

Chloe Robinson
Daryllyn Brooks

CONTENTS

1. GETTING STARTED

Getting Started

This unit is an orientation and provides the information you need to successfully learn from the instruction provided here. Though we do not talk about digital accessibility in this unit, it is still important to read through it.

> **Key Point:** Here the main focus is on **digital accessibility**. We may use the word "accessibility" on its own, which in the context of the discussion here should be interpreted as meaning "digital accessibility."

This Resource Will Be Helpful to...

Managers

This resource is aimed primarily at those who are responsible for implementing accessibility at an organizational level. These people tend to be **managers,** but may also be accessibility specialists, whose role it is to oversee the implementation of accessibility strategies and awareness throughout an organization.

Web Developers

Web developers may also wish to read the materials here to expand their understanding of the organizational aspects of implementing accessibility, thereby extending their role to that of an IT accessibility specialist, who is often the person to lead the implementation of accessibility culture in an organization.

Everyone Else

While managers and web developers are the primary audience here, anyone who has an interest in the aspects of implementing accessibility culture in an organization will find the materials informative.

Choosing Your Learning Path

A variety of elements have been added throughout the materials here to aid your learning. These are described here.

Your Accessibility Toolkit

Throughout the content, we've identified elements that should be added to the Accessibility Toolkit you will be assembling as you keep reading. These elements will include links to resource documents and online tools, as well as software or browser plugins that you may need to install or introduce to your staff. These will be identified in a green Toolkit box like the following:

> **Toolkit:** Provides useful tools and resources for your future reference.

Technical Details

Though the instruction here has been developed without much of the technical details of accessibility, there are places throughout the content where important technical information has been included. These details are contained in the blue Technical boxes. It's a good idea for those managing web accessibility efforts to be aware of some key technical elements of implementing digital accessibility, so they understand what technical staff should know.

> **Technical:** Aimed more at technical staff, typically containing HTML code samples.

Key Points

Important or notable information will be highlighted and labelled in Key Point boxes such as the one that follows. These will include "must know" information.

> **Key Point:** "Must know" information and interesting points.

Try This

Try This boxes contain activities designed to get you thinking or to give you first-hand experience with something you've just read about.

> **Try This:** Typically a short interactive exercise.

Readings & References

> **Readings & References:** These boxes provide links to various web resources for *optional* reading on the topics being discussed.

Self Tests

These short tests are included throughout the units to help you reinforce what you are learning.

> **Try This:** Skip ahead to the end and read through the Content Recap for a high-level summary of the topics covered here.

Final Project

The Final Project is writing a digital accessibility policy. Copy the template of topics listed below and paste them into the policy document you will develop. As you progress through the materials here, the readings and activities will provide information that you can use to help write the content for the document.

Project Details

A digital accessibility policy should be written as a guide or set of instructions that management and staff can refer to when they need to understand what they should be doing to meet the organization's accessibility requirements.

The following is a list of potential sections for the policy document. You can start with these and make the following changes and additions: add or remove sections or subsections; provide text for each section explaining the what, how, and/or who the section of the policy applies to; and organize it in a coherent way.

Key Point:

Template of Topics for Your Digital Accessibility Policy

- Background
- Company commitment
- Accessibility committee
    - Scope and responsibilities
    - Authority and enforcement
    - Support
- Guidelines and standards
    - Website development
    - Web content
    - Documents and communications
    - Multimedia
    - Third-party content
- Hiring equity and employment accommodation
- Training and awareness
- Digital accessibility resources
- Procurement
- Accessibility auditing and quality assurance
- Monitoring and periodic reviews
- Reporting
- Policy review

Accessibility Statement

Though we attempt to make all elements of this resource conform with international accessibility guidelines, we must acknowledge a few accessibility issues that are out of our control.

- Some external resources may not conform with accessibility guidelines.
- Third-party video content may not be captioned or may be captioned poorly.
- PDFs included in the web-based version of this resource have been tested with Acrobat Pro for accessibility, though will be inaccessible to those without the Acrobat Reader application installed on their computer.

Accessibility Tips for Web-Based Version

- Search for the "Skip to content" link at the start of each page when navigating by keyboard, and follow it to jump directly to the main content of the page.
- Links to external sites will always open in a new window.
- Use your screen reader's list headings feature to navigate through the headings within the content of a page.
- Use the "Previous Section" and "Next Section" links found at the bottom of each page to navigate through the sequence of pages. To access these links most easily, use your screen reader's landmarks list to jump to the navigation region, then press Tab and Shift-Tab to move between the next and previous links.
- Depending on the operating system and browser being used, font size can be adjusted by pressing a key combination including the plus (+) and minus (-) keys. On Windows systems, this is typically "CTRL+" and on Mac "Command+".

2. UNDERSTANDING THE BIG PICTURE

Understanding the Big Picture

This unit provides an overview of elements in digital accessibility culture, as well as background information to provide context for what you will learn about in the units that follow. You will develop a big picture of digital accessibility culture. This knowledge will act as a framework in which you will assemble key materials and resources as you progress through the content.

WHAT DOES ACCESSIBILITY MEAN TO YOUR BUSINESS?

In the following video from the Whitby Chamber of Commerce, four local Durham region and Toronto business owners tell us what accessibility means to their businesses. (**Note**: The captions for this video no longer seem to be working.)

Video: What does accessibility mean to your business?

A YouTube element has been excluded from this version of the text. You can view it online here: https://pressbooks.library.ryerson.ca/dabp/?p=630

Objectives and Activities

Objectives

By the end of this unit, you should be able to:

- Describe a variety of business cases for digital accessibility.
- Identify different types of disability and potential digital barriers experienced by people with each.
- Compare how accessibility laws are being introduced around the world.

Activities

- Write a convincing elevator pitch, lasting no longer than one minute.

The Sharp Clothing Company

The narrative here revolves around the story of "The Sharp Clothing Company" who recently received a complaint about the accessibility of their online store, which included a threat to take legal action if the company does not address the issue in a reasonable amount of time. This complaint came as a surprise to the company, who thought they were compliant with local accessibility laws, having recently retrofitted several of their retail locations to accommodate wheelchair access. However, they did not consider digital accessibility.

The company currently has twelve stores across Ontario and Quebec located primarily in shopping malls, and a distribution centre where clothing imported from around the world is distributed to physical stores and out to customers purchasing online. The head office is located in central Toronto.

The company has been growing rapidly, opening about two new stores per year since going public in 2012, with 222 people currently employed, across a broad range of roles. The company is making plans to expand into international markets in the coming year.

OTHER COMPANY DETAILS

- Business: Sales and distribution of economical clothing
- Established: 2002 and publicly traded since 2012
- Union status: Non-unionized
- Annual revenue in 2016: $46.5 million
- Marketing channels: Social media, website, television, newspapers, billboards, and print catalog

EMPLOYEES

Total number of employees: 222

- 8 senior managers
- 6 middle managers (at head office and distribution centre)
- 16 office staff
- 4 cleaning and maintenance staff
- 12 store managers
- 12 assistant store managers
- 100 in-store sales staff
- 8 communications and marketing staff
- 5 web developers
- 2 mobile app developers
- 2 user experience designers
- 5 web content authors
- 4 purchasers/buyers
- 8 24-hour telephone and online help staff

- 6 media support staff (videographer, photographer, and graphic artists, etc.)
- 24 distribution centre staff

YOUR ROLE

The complaint that was filed ended up with the company's CEO. She has come to you to handle the issue and tasks you to ensure that this type of complaint does not happen again. You already have a little background in accessibility, but it is primarily around customer service and design of physical spaces to accommodate people with disabilities. You gained this experience as the project manager during the company's efforts to make its stores accessible to people with disabilities. However, you have little experience with "digital accessibility" and have a limited technical background.

Your goal is to educate yourself about digital accessibility and implement a plan to address the complaint to ensure no other similar complaints occur. You have a budget which might cover hiring one or two additional staff members, training staff, updating technology, and launching promotional activities to raise awareness of digital accessibility throughout the company.

You will be working closely with other managers and specific staff in order to bring the company into compliance with digital accessibility laws, both locally and in the jurisdictions where the company is planning to do business.

As you progress through the reading and activities, you will be introduced to the various elements that need to be addressed in order to accomplish the company's compliance goals. In the final unit, you will assemble what you have learned into a *Digital Accessibility Policy for the Sharp Clothing Company*, a document that you can take away and ultimately use as a guide to implementing an accessibility plan for your own organization.

The Business Case for Accessibility

In 2011 and 2012, Karl Groves wrote an interesting series of articles that looked at the reality of business arguments for web accessibility. He points out that any argument needs to answer affirmatively to at least one of the following questions:

1. Will it make us money?
2. Will it save us money?
3. Will it reduce risk?

He outlines a range of potential arguments for accessibility:

- **Improved search engine optimization:** Customers will be able to find your site more easily because search engines can index it more effectively.
- **Improved usability:** Customers will have a more satisfying experience, thus spend more or return to your site more often.
- **Reduced website costs:** Developing to standard reduces bugs and interoperability issues, reducing development costs and problems integrating with other systems.
- **People with disabilities have buying power:** They won't spend if they have difficulty accessing your site; they will go to the competition that *does* place importance on accessibility.
- **Reduced resource utilization:** Building to standard reduces use of resources.
- **Support for low bandwidth:** If your site takes too long to load, people will go elsewhere.
- **Social responsibility:** Customers will come if they see you doing good for the world, and you are thinking of people with disabilities as full citizens.
- **Support for aging populations:** Aging populations also have money to spend and will come to your site over the less accessible, less usable competition.
- **Reduced legal risk:** You may be sued if you prevent equal access for citizens/customers or discriminate against people with disabilities.

What accessibility really boils down to is "quality of work," as Groves states. So, in approaching web accessibility, you may be better off not thinking so much in terms of reducing the risk of being sued, or losing customers because your site takes too long to load. Rather, the work you do is quality work, and the website you present to your potential customers is a quality website.

Video: The Business Case for Accessibility

A YouTube element has been excluded from this version of the text. You can view it online here: https://pressbooks.library.ryerson.ca/dabp/?p=639

Readings & References: If you'd like to learn more about business cases, here are a few references:

- Developing a Web Accessibility Business Case for Your Organization (W3C)
- Chasing the Web Accessibility Business Case (Karl Groves, 2012) part 1
- Chasing the Web Accessibility Business Case (Karl Groves, 2012) part 2
- Chasing the Web Accessibility Business Case (Karl Groves, 2012) conclusion
- 2 Seconds as the New Threshold of Acceptability for eCommerce Web Page Response Times (Akamai, 2009)
- Releasing Constraints: the impacts of increased accessibility on Ontario's economy (Summary)
- Releasing Constraints: Projecting the Economic Impacts of Increased Accessibility in Ontario (Full Report) [PDF]

AODA Background

Video: AODA Background

A YouTube element has been excluded from this version of the text. You can view it online here: https://pressbooks.library.ryerson.ca/dabp/?p=641

For readers from Ontario, Canada, we'll provide occasional references to the Accessibility for Ontarians with Disabilities Act (AODA). If you're studying here to work with accessibility outside Ontario, you may compare AODA's web accessibility requirements with those in your local area. They will be similar in many cases and likely based on the W3C WCAG 2.0 guidelines. The goal in Ontario is for all obligated organizations to meet the Level AA accessibility requirements of WCAG 2.0 by 2021, which, ultimately, is the goal of most international jurisdictions.

The AODA provided the motivation to create this resource. All businesses and organizations in Ontario with more than 50 employees (and all public sector organizations) are now required by law to make their websites accessible to people with disabilities (currently Level A). Many businesses still don't know what needs to be done in order to comply with the new rules, and this resource hopes to fill some of that need.

The AODA was passed as law in 2005, and, in July of 2011, the Integrated Accessibility Standards Regulation (IASR) brought together the five standards of the AODA, covering information and communication, employment, transportation, and design of public spaces, in addition to the original customer service standard.

The AODA sets out to make Ontario fully accessible by 2025, with an incremental roll-out of accessibility requirements over a period of 20 years. These requirements span a whole range of accessibility considerations, including physical spaces, customer service, the web, and much more.

Our focus here is on access to information, information technology (IT), and the web. The timeline set out in the AODA requires government and large organizations to remove all barriers in web content between 2012 and 2021. The timeline for these requirements is outlined in the table below. Any new or significantly updated information posted to the web must comply with the given level of accessibility by the given date. This includes both internet and intranet sites. Any content developed prior to January 1, 2012 is exempt.

	Level A	Level AA
Government	January 1, 2012 (except live captions and audio description)	January 1, 2016 (except live captions and audio description)
		January 1, 2020 (including live captions and audio description)
Designated Organizations*	Beginning January 1, 2014, **new** websites and significantly refreshed websites must meet Level A (except live captions and audio description)	January 1, 2021 (except live captions and audio description)

* Designated organizations means every municipality and every person or organization as outlined in the Public Service of Ontario Act 2006 Reg. 146/10, or private companies or organizations with 50 or more employees, in Ontario.

Key Point: The next key date for AODA designated organizations is January 1, 2021, when all web content must meet Level AA accessibility compliance.

Toolkit: Download and review the AODA Compliance Timelines [PDF].

Readings & References: For more about the AODA you can review the following references:

- Integrated Accessibility Standards Regulation (IASR/AODA)
- Reg. 146/10: Public Bodies and Commission Public Bodies – Definitions
- History of the Ontarians with Disabilities Act. (ODA) (David Lepofsky)

Video AODA: IASR: Information and Communications

A YouTube element has been excluded from this version of the text. You can view it online here: https://pressbooks.library.ryerson.ca/dabp/?p=641

Types of Disabilities and Associated Barriers

The Sharp Clothing Company recently completed upgrading all of its premises to include wheelchair access ramps, accessible washrooms, wheelchair-height customer service desks, and so on. The management was confident everything was done to meet accessibility standards, so they were surprised to receive a customer complaint about the company's online store being completely inaccessible by keyboard.

You have been asked to investigate the issue. After looking into the complaint you are surprised to find that there were many different types of disabilities and each one with its own accessibility challenges. You decide you need to learn more about how people with different disabilities use the web and digital information, since you see now there is more to accessibility than providing access for wheelchair users.

To understand where accessibility issues can arise, it is helpful to have a basic understanding of a range of disabilities and the related barriers found in digital content. These include:

- people who are blind
- people with low vision
- people who are deaf or hard of hearing
- people with mobility-related disabilities
- people with learning or cognitive disabilities

Not all people with disabilities encounter barriers in digital content, and **those with different types of disabilities encounter different types of barriers**. For instance, if a person is in a wheelchair, they may encounter no barriers at all in digital content. A person who is blind will experience different barriers than a person with limited vision. Many of the barriers that people with disabilities encounter on the web are often barriers found in electronic documents and multimedia. Different types of disabilities and some of their commonly associated barriers are described here.

Watch the following video to see how students with disabilities experience the Internet.

Video: Experiences of Students with Disabilities

A YouTube element has been excluded from this version of the text. You can view it online here: https://pressbooks.library.ryerson.ca/dabp/?p=643

In this video, David Berman talks about types of disabilities and their associated barriers.

Video: Web Accessibility Matters: Difficulties and Technologies: Avoiding Tradeoffs

A YouTube element has been excluded from this version of the text. You can view it online here: https://pressbooks.library.ryerson.ca/dabp/?p=643

People who Are Blind

People who are blind tend to face the most barriers in digital content, given the visual nature of much digital content. They will often use a screen reader to access their computer or device, and may use a refreshable Braille display to convert text to Braille.

Common barriers for this group include:

- Visual content that has no text alternative
- Functional elements that cannot be controlled with a keyboard
- Overly complex or excessive amounts of content
- Inability to navigate within a page of content
- Content that is not structured (i.e., missing proper headings)
- Inconsistent navigation
- Time limits (insufficient time to complete tasks)
- Unexpected actions (e.g., redirect when an element receives focus)
- Multimedia without audio description

For a quick look at how a person who is blind might use a screen reader like JAWS to navigate the web, watch the following video.

Video: Accessing the web using screen reading software

A YouTube element has been excluded from this version of the text. You can view it online here: https://pressbooks.library.ryerson.ca/dabp/?p=643

People with Low Vision

People with low vision are often able to see digital content if it is magnified. They may use a screen magnification program to increase the size and contrast of the content to make it more visible. They are less likely to use a screen reader than a person who is blind, though in some cases they will. People with low vision may rely on the magnification or text customization features in their web browser or word processor, or they may install other magnification or text reading software.

Common barriers for this group include:

- Content sized with non-resizable absolute measures
- Inconsistent navigation
- Images of text that degrade or pixelate when magnified
- Low contrast (inability to distinguish text from background)

- Time limits (insufficient time to complete tasks)
- Unexpected actions (e.g., redirect when an element receives focus)

See the following video for a description of some of the common barriers for people with low vision.

Video: Creating an accessible web (AD)

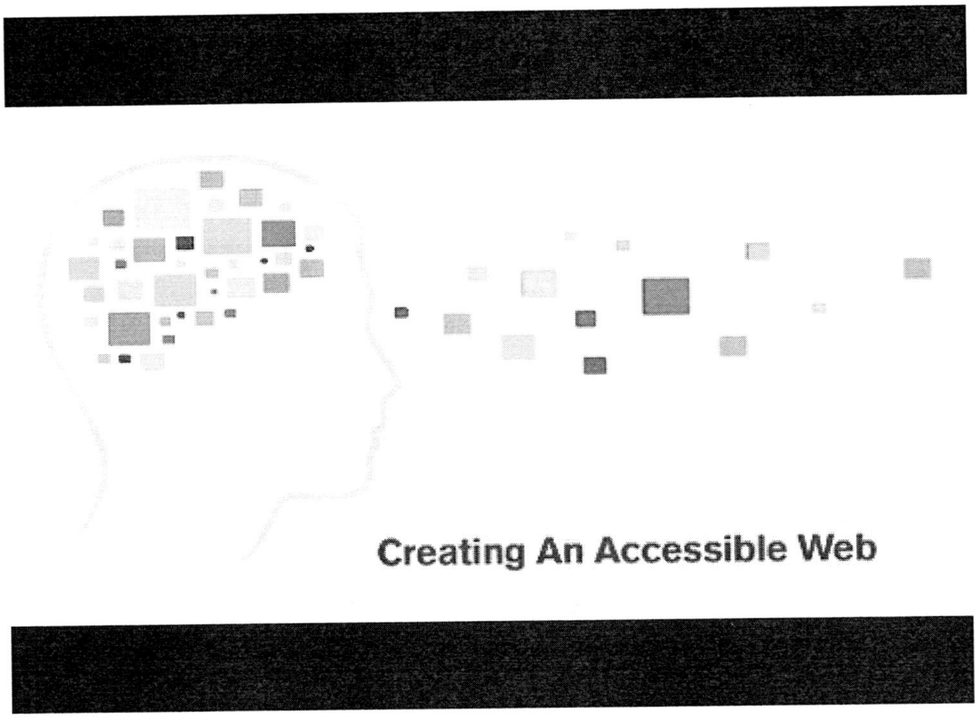

A YouTube element has been excluded from this version of the text. You can view it online here: https://pressbooks.library.ryerson.ca/dabp/?p=643

People who Are Deaf or Hard of Hearing

Most people who are deaf tend to face barriers where audio content is presented without text-based alternatives, and encounter relatively few barriers in digital content otherwise. Those who are deaf and blind will face many more barriers, including those described for people who are blind. For those who communicate with American Sign Language (ASL) or other sign languages (e.g., langue de Signes Quebecoise or LSQ), the written language of a website may produce barriers similar to those faced when reading in a second language.

Common barriers for this group include:

- Audio without a transcript
- Multimedia without captions or transcript

- Lack of ASL interpretation (for ASL/Deaf community)

People with Mobility-Related Disabilities

Mobility-related disabilities are quite varied. As mentioned earlier, one could be limited to a wheelchair for getting around, and face no significant barriers in digital content. Those who have limited use of their hands or who have fine-motor impairments that limit their ability to target and click elements in digital content with a mouse pointer, may not use a mouse at all. Instead, they might rely on a keyboard or perhaps their voice to control movement (i.e., speech recognition) through digital content along with switches to control mouse clicks.

Common barriers for this group include:

- Clickable areas that are too small
- Functional elements that cannot be controlled with a keyboard
- Time limits (insufficient time to complete tasks)

People with Learning or Cognitive Disabilities

Learning and cognitive-related disabilities can be as varied as mobility-related disabilities, perhaps more so. These disabilities can range from a mild reading related disability, to very severe cognitive impairments that may result in limited use of language and difficulty processing complex information. For most of the disabilities in this range, there are some common barriers, and others that only affect those with more severe cognitive disabilities.

Common barriers for this group include:

- Use of overly complex/advanced language
- Inconsistent navigation
- Overly complex or excessive amounts of content
- Time limits (insufficient time to complete tasks)
- Unstructured content (no visible headings, sections, topics, etc.)
- Unexpected actions (e.g., redirect when an element receives focus)

More specific disability-related issues include:

- Reading: Text justification (inconsistent spacing between words)
- Reading: Images of text (not readable with a text reader)
- Visual: Visual content with no text description
- Math: Images of math equations (not readable with a math reader)

Everyone

While we generally think of barriers in terms of access for people with disabilities, there are some barriers that impact all types of users, though these are often thought of in terms of usability. Usability and accessibility go hand-in-hand.

Adding accessibility features improves usability for others. Many people, including those who do not consider themselves to have a specific disability (such as those over the age of 50) may find themselves experiencing typical age-related loss of sight, hearing, or cognitive ability. Those with varying levels of colour blindness may also fall into this group.

Some of these usability issues include:

- Link text that does not describe the destination or function of the link
- Overly complex content
- Inconsistent navigation
- Low contrast
- Unstructured content

Try This: Experience colour blindness: Corbis Colour Blindness Simulation

Readings & References: To learn more about disabilities and associated barriers, read the following: How People with Disabilities Use the Web

North American Digital Accessibility Laws and Regulations

Knowing the lengths your company recently went to to ensure physical accessibility at the storefront locations, you are eager to gain an understanding about how accessibility legislation may extend into the digital realm. The added risk of potential legal action and reference to a human rights violation in the complaint has drawn concern from the company's leadership. They have asked you to investigate further into what legislation might already exist with reference to digital accessibility.

You discover that, in fact, there is legislation in place in Ontario as part of the Accessibility for Ontarians with Disabilities Act (AODA), specifically **Section 12** and **Section 14** that speak to digital accessibility, which cover accessible formats and web content, respectively. You see that, indeed, accessible websites are addressed in Section 14(4).

- AODA Section 12
- AODA Section 14

While you are reading about the AODA Information and Communications Standard, you remember the discussion at the last manager's meeting, about the plan coming together that will see several new stores open over the next year, located in the United States, the European Union, and Australia. It occurs to you that these countries may have their own digital accessibility standards, and that you should look into those while learning about the local accessibility requirements.

Web Content Accessibility Guidelines (WCAG 2.0)

The W3C Web Content Accessibility Guidelines (**WCAG 2.0**) has become broadly accepted as the definitive source for web accessibility rules around the world, with many jurisdictions adopting it verbatim, or with minor adjustments, as the basis for accessibility laws that remove discrimination against people with disabilities on the web.

While you do not need to read the whole WCAG 2.0 document, it is good to have a basic understanding of what it covers.

> **Toolkit: WCAG 2.0** can be dry, and time consuming to read through and understand. We have created the 10 Key Guidelines that summarizes and helps familiarize you with the more common web accessibility issues.

After reviewing the 10 Key Guidelines, start by learning about the Canadian and U.S. web accessibility regulations, then take the Challenge Test to check your knowledge.

Canada

ACCESSIBILITY FOR ONTARIANS WITH DISABILITIES ACT (AODA)

The materials here haqve been written in the context of the AODA, which came into effect in 2005 with the goal of making Ontario the most inclusive jurisdiction in the world by 2025. Part of this twenty-year rollout involved educating businesses in Ontario, many of which are now obligated by the Act to make their websites accessible, first at Level A between 2012 and 2014, and at Level AA between 2016 and 2021.

> **Key Point:** AODA adopts WCAG 2.0 for its Web accessibility requirements, with the exception of two guidelines:
>
> 1. Ontario businesses and organizations are not required to provide captioning for live web-based broadcasts (WCAG 2.0 Guideline 1.2.4, Level A)
> 2. Ontario businesses and organizations are not required to provide audio description for pre-recorded web-based video (WCAG 2.0 Guideline 1.2.5, Level AA)
>
> Otherwise, AODA adopts WCAG 2.0 verbatim.

> **Toolkit:** For key information on the adoption of WCAG 2.0 in the context of the AODA, refer to the Integrated Accessibility Standards (of the AODA).

CANADIAN GOVERNMENT STANDARD ON WEB ACCESSIBILITY

In 2011, the Government of Canada (GOC) introduced its most recent set of web accessibility standards, made up of four sub standards that replace the previous Common Look and Feel 2.0 standards. The Standard on Web Accessibility adopts WCAG 2.0 as its Web accessibility requirements with the exception of Guideline 1.4.5 Images of Text (Level AA) in cases where "essential images of text" are used, in cases where "demonstrably justified" exclusions are required, and for any archived Web content. The standard applies only to Government of Canada websites.

> **Toolkit:** Full details of Government of Canada accessibility requirements read the Standard on Web Accessibility.

ACCESSIBILITY 2024

In 2014 the British Columbia government released Accessibility 2024, a ten-year action plan designed around twelve building blocks intended to make the province the most progressive in Canada for people with disabilities. Accessible Internet is one of those building blocks. The aim is to have all B.C. government websites meet WCAG 2.0 AA requirements by the end of 2016.

CANADIANS WITH DISABILITIES ACT

Currently a work in progress, this act intends to produce national accessibility regulations for Canada. Visit the Barrier-Free Canada website for more about the developing Canadians with Disabilities Act, and the Government of Canada on the consultation process.

United States

AMERICANS WITH DISABILITIES ACT (ADA)

The ADA does not have any specific technical requirements upon which it requires websites to be accessible, however, there have been a number of cases where organizations that are considered to be "places of public accommodation" have been sued due to the inaccessibility of their websites (e.g., Southwest Airlines and AOL), where the defendant organization was required to conform with WCAG 2.0 Level A and Level AA guidelines.

There is a proposed revision to Title III of the ADA (Federal Register Volume 75, Issue 142, July 26, 2010) that would, if passed, require WCAG 2.0 Level A and AA conformance to make Web content accessible under ADA.

> **Readings & References:** Nondiscrimination on the Basis of Disability; Accessibility of Web Information and Services of State and Local Government Entities and Public Accommodations

SECTION 508 (OF THE REHABILITATION ACT, U.S.)

Section 508 is part of the U.S. Rehabilitation Act and its purpose is to eliminate barriers in information technology, applying to all Federal Agencies that develop, procure, maintain, or use electronic and information technology. Any company that sells to the U.S. Government must also provide products and services that comply with the eleven accessibility guidelines Section 508 describes in Section 1194.22 of the Act.

These guidelines were originally based on a subset of the WCAG 1.0 guidelines, and were recently updated to include WCAG 2.0 Level A and AA guidelines as new requirements for those obligated through Section 508. Though in effect as of March 20, 2017, those affected by the regulation are required to comply with the updated regulation by **January 18, 2018**.

> **Readings & References:**
>
> - US Web Accessibility Law Summary
> - Section 508 Refresh (Jan 18, 2018)
> - Section 508 – 1194.22 (Current)
> - Comparison Table of WCAG 2.0 to Existing 508 Standards
> - Section 508 Proposed Update (February 18, 2015 – See section B of Major Issues)

Self-Test 1

1. In Ontario, which section of the AODA Information and Communication Standards addresses website and web content accessibility?
    1. Section 6
    2. Section 12
    3. Section 13
    4. Section 14
    5. Section 18
2. In the United States, when are obligated organizations required to comply with the recent changes to Section 508 of the Rehabilitation Act?
    1. January 1, 2019
    2. January 1, 2018
    3. January 18, 2018
    4. March 17, 2017
    5. January 1, 2017

Answer Key to Challenge Test 1

An interactive or media element has been excluded from this version of the text. You can view it online here: https://pressbooks.library.ryerson.ca/dabp/?p=654

International Digital Accessibility Regulations

United Kingdom

EQUALITY ACT 2010

The Equality Act in the United Kingdom does not specifically address how web accessibility should be implemented, but in Section 29(1), require that those who sell or provide services to the public must not discriminate against any person requiring the service. Effectively, preventing a person with a disability from accessing a service on the web constitutes discrimination.

Sections 20 and 29(7) of the Act make it an ongoing duty of service providers to make "reasonable adjustments" to accommodate people with disabilities. To this end, the British Standards Institution (BSI) provides a code of practice (BS 8878) on web accessibility, based on WCAG 1.0.

For more about BSI efforts, watch the following video:

Video: BSI Documentary – Web accessibility – World Standards Day 14 Oct 2010

A YouTube element has been excluded from this version of the text. You can view it online here: https://pressbooks.library.ryerson.ca/dabp/?p=656

Readings & References:

- Website accessibility and the Equality Act 2010
- Equality Act 2010
- Equality Act 2010: Guidance

Europe

Throughout Europe, a number of countries have their own accessibility laws, each based on WCAG 2.0. In 2010, the European Union itself introduced web accessibility guidelines based on WCAG 2.0 Level AA requirements. The EU Parliament passed a law in 2014 that requires all public sector websites, and private sector websites that provide key public services, to conform with WCAG 2.0 Level AA requirements, with new content conforming within one year, existing content conforming within three years, and multimedia content conforming within five years.

This does not mean, however, that all countries in the EU must now conform. The law now goes before the EU Council, where heads of state will debate it, which promises to draw out adoption for many years into the future, if it gets adopted at all.

Readings & References:

- The EU Internet Handbook: Web Accessibility
- New European Standard on accessibility requirements for public procurement of ICT products and services (ETSI EN 301 549)
- Standard – EN 301 549

ITALY

In Italy, the Stanca Act 2004 (*Disposizioni per favorire l'accesso dei soggetti disabili agli strumenti informatici*) governs web accessibility requirements for all levels of government, private firms that are licensees of public services, public assistance and rehabilitation agencies, transport and telecommunications companies, as well as ICT service contractors.

The Stanca Act has 22 technical accessibility requirements originally based on WCAG 1.0 Level A guidelines, updated in 2013 to reflect changes in WCAG 2.0.

Readings & References:

- Stanca 2013 Requirements (Italian)

GERMANY

In Germany, BITV 2.0 (*Barrierefreie Informationstechnik-Verordnung*), which adopts WCAG 2.0 with a few modifications, requires accessibility for all government websites at Level AA (i.e., BITV Priority 1).

Readings & References:

- BITV (Appendix 1)

FRANCE

Accessibility requirements in France are specified in Law No 2005-102, Article 47, and its associated technical requirements are defined in RGAA 3 (based on WCAG 2.0). It is mandatory for all public online communication services, public institutions, and the State, to conform with RGAA (WCAG 2.0).

Readings & References:

- Law No 2005-102, Article 47 (French)
- Référentiel Général d'Accessibilité pour les Administrations (RGAA) (French)

SPAIN

The web accessibility laws in Spain are Law 34/2002 and Law 51/2003, which require all government websites to conform with WCAG 1.0 Priority 2 guidelines. More recently, UNE 139803:2012 adopts WCAG 2.0 requirements and mandates that the following types of organizations comply with WCAG Level AA requirements: government and government-funded organizations; organizations larger than 100 employees; organizations with a trading column greater than 6 million Euros; or organizations providing financial, utility, travel/passenger, or retail services online.

(See: Legislation in Spain)

Readings & References:

- Law 34/2002 – Information Society and Electronic Commerce Services Act PDF (Spanish)
- Law 34/2002 – Information Society and Electronic Commerce Services Act web page (Spanish)
- UNE 139803:2004 – Applications for people with disabilities (Spanish)
- UNE 139803:2012 – Web content accessibility requirements. (supersedes 139803:2004)
- Law 51/2003 – Equality of opportunities, non-discrimination, and universal accessibility for people with disabilities (Spanish)

AUSTRALIA

Though not specifically referencing the web, section 24 of the Disability Discrimination Act of 1992 makes it unlawful for a person who provides goods, facilities, or services to discriminate on the grounds of disability. This law was tested in 2000, when a blind man successfully sued the Sydney Organizing Committee for the Olympic Games (SOCOG) when its website prevented him from purchasing event tickets.

The Australian Human Rights and Equal Opportunity Commission (HREOC) shortly after released the World Wide Web Access: Disability Discrimination Act Advisory Notes. These were last updated in 2014, and, while they do not have direct legal force, they do provide web accessibility guidance for Australians on how to avoid discriminatory practices when developing web content, based on WCAG 2.0.

Readings & References:

- World Wide Web Access: Disability Discrimination Act Advisory Notes

Readings & References: For more about international web accessibility laws, see the following resources:

- Chapter 17 – Web Accessibility (2006)
- Policies Relating to Web Accessibility (W3C)
- Government accessibility standards and WCAG 2
- World Laws WebAIM

Activity: One-Minute Elevator Pitch

Establishing a culture of accessibility in an organization requires buy-in from senior management. These managers may not always understand the implications of accessibility barriers on the company. Using the knowledge you have gained to this point, write an elevator pitch to convince a senior manager that accessibility is important to the company.

If you are not familiar with elevator pitches, they often unfold when you, the speaker, getting on the elevator, happen to run into a key senior person in the company, who typically spends her day running from meeting to meeting. You have her as a captive audience for one minute while the elevator ascends. This is the only opportunity you will have to pitch your idea to this person, and if you succeed in convincing this person, she will support you in your effort.

Your task in this activity is to convince one of the following people that digital accessibility is very important and you have a good idea that is sure to benefit the company. You may want to consider different arguments to convince different people.

- President/Chief Executive Officer
- Director of Marketing
- IT Manager/Chief Information Officer
- General Manager
- Human Resource Director

For help with creating your elevator pitch, read Mindtools's How to Create an Elevator Pitch.

Suggested Viewing: If you would like to see examples of an elevator pitch, have a look through the following video resources.

1. Video: 6 Elevator Pitches for the 21st Century

A YouTube element has been excluded from this version of the text. You can view it online here: https://pressbooks.library.ryerson.ca/dabp/?p=658

2. Video: Elevator Pitch Winner (Utah State)

A YouTube element has been excluded from this version of the text. You can view it online here: https://pressbooks.library.ryerson.ca/dabp/?p=658

3. Video: Sarah Bourne Makes the Business Case for Implementing Accessible Technology

A YouTube element has been excluded from this version of the text. You can view it online here: https://pressbooks.library.ryerson.ca/dabp/?p=658

4. Video: Mike Paciello Makes the Business Case for Implementing Accessible Technology

A YouTube element has been excluded from this version of the text. You can view it online here: https://pressbooks.library.ryerson.ca/dabp/?p=658

Understanding the Big Picture: Takeaways

In this unit, you learned that:

- When a business addresses digital accessibility, it actually saves money and doing so is not a non-recoverable cost to the business.
- There is a strong potential for a significant increase in customers [illegible] businesses that address digital accessibility.
- Digital accessibility should not be an afterthought, rather it needs to be part of the business strategy and the daily operations of the business.
- Addressing accessibility is a quality attribute of a business and improves its profile.

3. THE COMMITTEE AND THE CHAMPION

The Committee and the Champion

If your organization has more than a handful of employees, or has multiple groups or departments that serve different purposes within the organization, it is helpful to recruit staff to represent and speak for each group on an Accessibility Committee (or whatever you choose to call it). These will typically be comprised of people in senior positions, people with influence, and employees with disabilities. These committee members must be willing to sell the ideas put forth by the committee to raise awareness and affect the culture within the group they represent.

You will probably also want to assign a person to be in charge of the whole committee: A person we will refer to as the Accessibility Champion. This person should have expertise in the accessibility area, be able to lead, manage change, and oversee the organization's accessibility efforts as a whole.

Objectives and Activities

Objectives

By the end of this unit, you should be able to:

- Distinguish accessibility skills and knowledge required across a variety of roles.
- Outline the makeup of an Accessibility Committee.
- Describe important characteristics of a good Accessibility Champion.

Activities

- Assess your own ability to be an Accessibility Champion.

Identifying Key Areas and People

Having learned about how people with disabilities use digital content and the Web, and knowing about the local and international digital accessibility regulations, you now want to determine what led to the customer's complaint in the first place.

The person who submitted the complaint has identified that he is blind and uses a technology called a screen reader to access content on the Web. From your research on how people with disabilities use the Web, you know that screen readers read out the text content from web pages.

The complaint mentions two particular issues. First, many images in the shopping area of the company's website are announced as file names, such as "rt-004.jpg", rather than something meaningful like "add to shopping cart." You discover the problem is the result of images in the shopping cart application not having a text description. You know that "alt text" is the way to provide a text description for images on the Web.

Second, the buttons in the shopping cart cannot be activated with a key press; rather, they require a person to click the buttons with a mouse. Since people who are blind typically cannot use a mouse (not being able to see a mouse pointer), you have learned that they usually rely on their keyboard to navigate through content and to press buttons or activate links. When these website elements cannot be accessed or operated with a key press, they are inaccessible to anyone who relies on a keyboard to navigate.

You first approach the content developer who set up the products in the shopping cart application, and ask that she go through the product list and add the missing text descriptions. But, she tells you the shopping cart editor does not have a way to add text descriptions, or alt text, for product images.

You then approach your company's web developer to see if it is possible to add an alt text field to the editor used to add product images. As it turns out, the shopping cart application is a third-party proprietary application, and, apart from simple changes to brand the shopping cart, there is little that can be done to make changes to the editor without going back to the vendor. You also ask your web developer about the keyboard access problem, and he tells you this cannot be modified either without going back to the vendor.

You wonder how the company ended up purchasing this shopping cart application given its limited accessibility support. The next stop in your investigation is your purchasing department. You ask about the accessibility requirements that were included with the request for proposals (RFP), and discover that no accessibility requirements were outlined in the RFP. The purchasing department did not know about the requirement to purchase accessible technologies when they are available.

Through this investigation, you begin to realize that accessibility knowledge needs to be weaved through many roles in the company. The next area you focus on is understanding what types of digital accessibility knowledge is needed for various roles in the company, and the potential training that might be needed to ensure various roles understand their accessibility responsibilities.

The roles you identify include:

- Retail store staff
- Retail store managers and assistant managers
- Web developers
- Web content editors
- Communications and marketing staff
- Procurement and purchasing staff
- Telephone support staff
- Video support staff
- Graphic artists
- Senior managers and directors
- Human resource staff
- Distribution centre staff
- Office support staff

Depending on a person's role in a company, different types of accessibility knowledge may be needed. The following is an example of the different knowledge various roles may need, though depending on the size of a company and the nature of the business, this knowledge could be adapted across roles. For instance, if a company does not have a human resource (HR) department, then knowledge of accessible hiring practices and accessibility knowledge requirements for various roles may shift to senior managers responsible for hiring new staff.

Retail store staff: Since retail staff often do not use digital tools or content beyond perhaps a web-based checkout, the main focus of their knowledge should be disability sensitivity, so they are able to interact comfortably and appropriately when people with disabilities are shopping in the retail stores.

People are often unsure how to interact with a person with a disability, if they have little experience with it. They may feel uncomfortable and wary of saying the wrong thing. In general, people with disabilities should be treated like anyone else, though this may be difficult for some, for instance, who have never met a person who is blind or deaf or uses a wheelchair.

Retail store managers and assistant managers: Like other retail store staff, store managers should also receive disability sensitivity training, and they should be able to provide training to other store staff.

Managers should also have a general overview of the business's accessibility requirements as a whole, so they are able to identify and potentially resolve any accessibility issues they may encounter through the day-to-day retail store operation.

Web developers: The company's web developers play a key role in ensuring that the company's public website, in particular meets accessibility requirements. They should have a good understanding of the W3C Web Content Accessibility Guidelines (WCAG 2.0), in addition to having expert knowledge of HTML, CSS, and JavaScript. WCAG is the international guideline for developing accessible web content and is the basis for many international web accessibility regulations.

A web developer may also be a good person to oversee the company's digital accessibility efforts, as they have a good understanding of the technologies involved and the ability to evaluate and remediate accessibility issues. An accessibility lead should have both understanding of accessibility technology, and an understanding of disability and related accessibility barriers. This combination of expertise can be difficult to find, so it would be more effective to educate a web developer on disability and accessibility issues than training a disability expert on the technical aspects of implementing digital accessibility.

Web content editors: Those who develop the content for a website should have basic understanding of WCAG 2.0, though they typically do not need the level of understanding that web developers need. Among the many potential accessibility issues in digital content, web content editors should be aware of things like including text descriptions for images, structuring content with the proper use of headings, and creating links in content that describe in a meaningful way where the link leads.

Communications and marketing staff: Marketing staff should also have the basic understanding of WCAG that content editors have, though there are some other guidelines that may be relevant, such as effective use of colour when developing promotional materials (e.g., having sufficient contrast between foreground and background and ensuring that colour alone is not used to represent meaning).

Marketing staff may also produce documents that are distributed both internally and externally to the public. They should also have an understanding of how to use accessibility features in various document authoring tools such as Microsoft Word or Adobe Acrobat Pro, among others. Most current document authoring tools should have features for testing and authoring accessible documents. Upgrades may be necessary to take advantage of those features, if older software is still being used.

Procurement and purchasing staff: Those who buy products and resources for a company need to have a good understanding of WCAG 2.0, or at a minimum understand that when purchasing, software in particular, and choosing between comparable products, the more accessible one should be purchased. Purchasing agents may make use of third party accessibility evaluation services to report on the accessibility of potential purchases. The company's web developers may also be a good source for evaluators, assuming they have acquired the necessary expertise with WCAG.

Procurement staff also need to know how to ask for accessibility features from vendors and how to critically evaluate the responses to those requests, ensuring vendors are being honest about the accessibility of their products. Some vendors may tell you what you want to hear, which may not necessarily be the whole truth, while others may not know about accessibility, which is a good indication that there products are not accessible.

Telephone support staff: These staff should have similar disability sensitivity training, though typically, unless a person identifies themselves as having a disability, they may not be aware of such facts. Nonetheless, if they are interacting with a person they know to have a disability, they need to know how to interact in an acceptable way.

Telephone support staff should know how to use a TTY (Teletype or Teletypewriter), used by people who are deaf to communicate with hearing individuals by phone. If your support services do not include TTY access, telecommunications providers can typically provide the service.

Video support staff: Video production editors need to know about captioning and audio description. Captioning provides access to the audio track in multimedia content for those who are deaf, and audio description provides access to meaningful visual elements or activity in a video that are not obvious by listening to the audio track, for those who are blind.

Graphic artists: Similar to marketing staff, graphic artists need to be aware of the basic WCAG guidelines and issues around the use of colour.

Senior managers and directors: The senior people in a company need to have a basic understanding of digital accessibility as a whole, as well as a good understanding of the accessibility regulations that govern a business's accessibility requirements. They also need to be open to change and to understand the business arguments for creating an inclusive business. Ultimately, it is the senior management in a company that make or break a company's accessibility efforts.

Human resource staff: HR staff need to have a good understanding of the local accessibility laws, and related accessible hiring practices. They also need to know about the required accessibility knowledge for the roles described here, as well as other potential roles. HR staff also need to be able to ask the right questions to determine, for instance, if a web developer has expertise with WCAG, or to perhaps assess the marketing department or office personnel's understanding of accessibility features in the authoring tools they use.

HR staff may also be responsible for training efforts. While having accessibility knowledge for a given role should give applicants an advantage over others, in reality it is often difficult to find candidates with both expert understanding of the job they are being hired for, and knowledge of accessibility elements for that role. Fortunately, for many roles, accessibility training is often quick, like training office staff to use PDF accessibility features. With a few hours of training, staff can acquire all the skills they need to get started creating accessible content. However, for other roles, like web developers, it can take a significant amount of training and time to develop their expertise.

Distribution centre staff: These staff members may need little accessibility training. These people may include inventory control staff, a shipper/receiver, truck drivers, or a warehouse manager, among others. They may have no interaction with the public, and may not be involved in activities that produce digital content, but should be aware of their company's accessibility obligations.

Office support staff: These staff members are likely to use various document authoring tools, and should be aware of, and use, the accessibility features tools such as Microsoft Word and Acrobat Acrobat Pro provide.

Establishing an Accessibility Committee

Understanding the diversity of skills and knowledge in the company's workforce, you decide that it will be more effective if each department managed their own digital accessibility efforts. You decide to create an accessibility committee, made up of senior or influential people from each of the major groups in the company. Your goal is to take a proactive approach to accessibility, addressing issues before they become complaints, rather than a reactive approach, where issues are addressed only when a complaint has been received.

By implementing a proactive approach, you are aiming to address potential barriers before they result in lost customers. While the company did receive a complaint, you understand that many people who encounter accessibility barriers do not complain. They just leave, perhaps going to the competition. You are convinced that if they come to your website and have a pleasant, accessible experience, they will likely return and make additional purchases.

You plan to have the accessibility committee initially meet several times over a two month period, to get accessibility efforts underway, then reduce the frequency of meetings to once per quarter, to receive updates from each group and discuss any new issues that arise.

Who Should be on the Committee?

Ideally the Accessibility Committee (AC) should be made up of influential and knowledgeable representatives from different areas of the company, starting with a senior executive who can affect the company's accessibility policy. In Figure 2.1, the CEO at the top of the organizational structure would be that person, though it does not necessarily need to be the company's top officer.

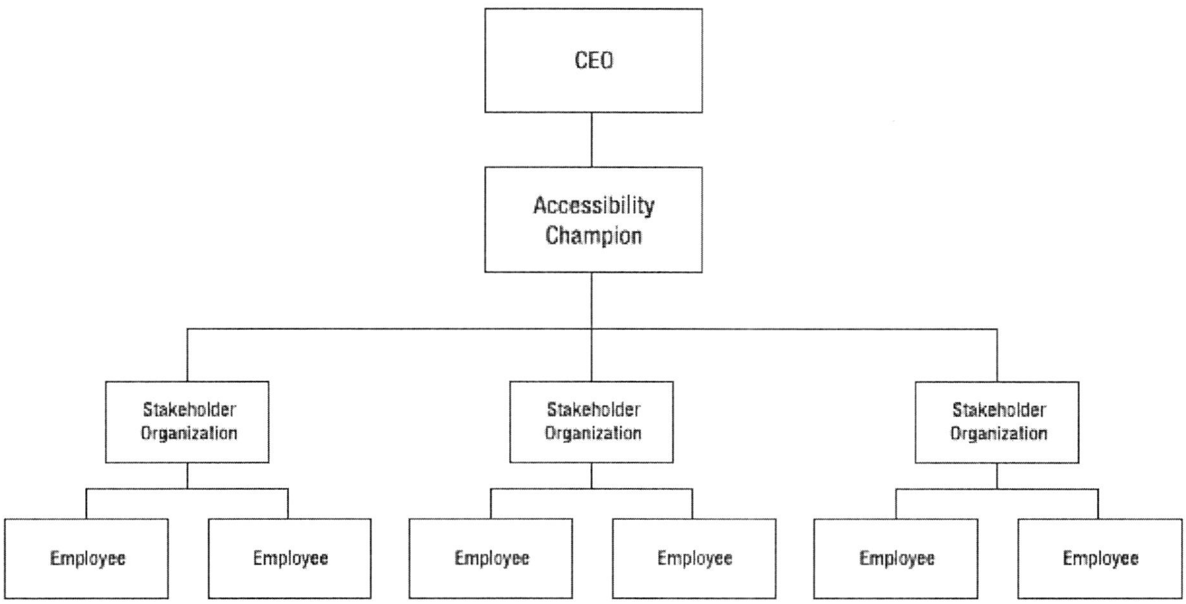

Figure 2.1: A possible accessibility committee structure
Source: *Web Accessibility: Web Standards and Regulatory Compliance*, Chapter 3: Implementing Accessibility in the Enterprise. (Urban Burks, 2006)

Below the senior executive is the person who will oversee the committee, in this case referred to as the "Accessibility Champion." This person should be in a relatively senior position, or have substantial influence in the company, who has a good understanding of accessibility, disability, and the technical aspects of implementing accessibility. This person should also find accessibility interesting and challenging, and should not be forced into the role. Depending on the size of the company, it may be a person dedicated specifically to overseeing the company's accessibility efforts, or it could be someone in another role who manages accessibility efforts on a part-time basis.

You debate whether you are the best person to take on the Accessibility Champion role. While you are becoming more familiar with digital accessibility, and you find it very interesting, you are not sure if you have the technical knowledge to fully understand the possibilities or options for developing and implementing digital accessibility. For now, you take on the role yourself, but leave the option open to assign the role to another member of the accessibility committee once it has been established, or even look outside the company for a person with the right balance of technical background and disability/accessibility knowledge to understand the technologies involved.

You decide to approach the CEO, who originally asked you to investigate the complaint, and ask her if she would be a member of the committee. She agrees, but suggests that after initially establishing the committee, she will pass that role to the senior VP. You also approach the director of retail sales, who oversees the retail managers and visits retail stores regularly. You also ask the IT manager to participate, as well as one of the senior web developers who reports to him and who has some web accessibility experience.

ACCESSIBILITY COMMITTEE MEMBERS

- CEO (president)
- You (project manager)
- Director of retail sales
- IT manager
- HR manager
- Senior web developer
- The senior VP (oversees operations at head office)
- Director of marketing (oversees the video editors and graphic artists)

Other members of the accessibility committee are strategically selected from throughout the company, with the aim of including representatives across all areas of the company where digital accessibility is a concern, as well as those known to be knowledgeable on the subject of digital accessibility, which may include people within the company who have disabilities.

Accessibility Committee Goals and Responsibilities

Clear goals for the accessibility committee should be defined and promoted throughout an organization so that everyone understands the committee's function.

The accessibility committee should be responsible for:

- Raising accessibility awareness
- Encouraging feedback to share problems and solutions
- Implementing quality assurance procedures
- Consulting on legal matters related to accessibility
- Providing web and digital accessibility support
- Developing internal accessibility standards
- Representing the organization in accessibility-related public affairs

Source: *Implementing Accessibility in the Enterprise*, pp. 73-74

Readings & References:

- Municipal Accessibility Advisory Committees

Self-Test 2

1. Of the following roles, which roles need a good understanding of WCAG 2.0, as opposed to a basic understanding? Choose all that apply.
   1. Graphic artists
   2. Web developers
   3. Web content editors
   4. Video support staff
   5. Procurement and purchasing staff
   6. Retail store staff
2. Which of the following should be goals and responsibilities of an accessibility committee? Choose all that apply.
   1. Planning the annual company golf tournament
   2. Raising accessibility awareness
   3. Representing the organization in public affairs related to accessibility
   4. Encouraging feedback to share problems and solutions
   5. Developing internal accessibility standards
   6. Implementing accessibility in quality assurance procedures
   7. Consulting on legal matters related to accessibility
   8. Providing web and digital accessibility support

Answer Key to Challenge Test 2

An interactive or media element has been excluded from this version of the text. You can view it online here: https://pressbooks.library.ryerson.ca/dabp/?p=677

Characteristics of a Digital Accessibility Champion

The Accessibility Champion will be the person who leads an organization's accessibility efforts. The title may vary from organization to organization, though the role will be the same.

The Accessibility Champion should be able to relate to others at their level. For instance, when working with developers to promote accessibility practices, being able to talk to them with appropriate technical language will help get the message across convincingly. Similarly, when working with designers, this person should be able to talk in terms of Universal Design and Inclusive Design practices.

Though an Accessibility Champion does not necessarily need to have formal computer science or design backgrounds, knowledge in these areas is important to be effective in the role. At a minimum, the Champion needs to be comfortable working with technology, and have a good understanding of how people with disabilities access information and digital content.

The Accessibility Champion should have a particular set of necessary, and desirable characteristics, described here:

Necessary Characteristics

- Has the ability to lead
- Can influence people at all levels of authority, and across all roles
- Has strong communication skills (verbal and written) and the ability to motivate people
- Is creative when faced with challenging situations
- Can talk about disability issues in an informed way
- Is familiar with a range of assistive technologies
- Understands the societal effects of inclusion
- Is passionate about inclusive design
- Has a strong technical background

Desirable Characteristics

- Is able to teach
- Is able to present convincingly to small or large audiences
- Has a disability or is closely related to someone with a disability

- Is a software engineer, or programmer
- Is a web developer
- Is a user interface or interaction designer

Activity: To Be or Not to Be the Accessibility Champion

Playing the role of the Digital Accessibility Project Manager, one of your decisions will be who takes on the role of the Accessibility Champion. You could very well be the Champion, but do you have the characteristics to take on this role?

Using the "Characteristics of a Digital Accessibility Champion," how many of the characteristics do you possess? How many are you lacking? What skills could you learn to make you better suited for the role? Are there other characteristics of a champion you have that are not mentioned?

The Committee and the Champion: Takeaways

In this unit, you learned that:

- Disability sensitivity training and a good understanding of accessibility and standards, such as WCAG accessibility barriers, are all key knowledge areas required in different company roles.
- Accessibility committee members should be chosen strategically and should represent a good cross section of the business.

4. CREATING DIGITAL ACCESSIBILITY CULTURE

Creating Digital Accessibility Culture

Digital Accessibility Culture Defined

"Culture," in the context of digital accessibility, refers to an overarching consciousness or awareness throughout an organization of potential barriers – barriers that may prevent people with disabilities from participating in digital activities or consuming digital information at the same level as their fully able peers.

It means that attention to accessibility is weaved into an organization's processes and integrated with quality assurance, so, when products and services are evaluated, accessibility is part of that evaluation. Everyone who is involved in producing products or delivering services has accessibility in mind while they carry out their duties. They know how to address accessibility in their work, and, if they encounter potential barriers they are not sure of, they ask questions, perhaps, addressing questions to accessibility experts on staff or to the Web or third-party experts to search out answers. In short, they will persevere until they find a solution.

Developing digital accessibility culture requires buy-in from the most senior executive in an organization. That buy-in trickles down through an organization, influencing senior managers, who influence junior managers, who influence the staff reporting to them, and so on, flowing all the way down the organizational hierarchy.

This culture, by way of its adoption throughout an organization, becomes a practice that guides business activities in designing and developing new products, to production, to service delivery, to marketing and communications, to procurement, to hiring, and more. All aspects of the organization are influenced by attention to digital accessibility inclusion.

Objectives and Activities

Objectives

By the end of this unit, you should be able to:

- Assess an organization's current level of digital accessibility.
- Describe strategies for building awareness of digital accessibility.
- Plan staff-training strategies for different areas of the organization.
- Explain strategies for managing resistance and change.

Activities

- Handling Resistance

Assessing an Organization's Current Digital Accessibility Status

One of the the accessibility committee's first tasks is to determine where the company is in terms of its compliance with accessibility guidelines and to identify gaps where improvements are needed. Since you do not have an accessibility expert on staff, you decide to look into firms that provide accessibility auditing services.

Choosing an Accessibility Auditor

Unless there is already an accessibility expert on staff, organizations likely want to hire a third-party auditor or find a person to hire on as one.

It is typically easier to find an auditing service than to find an accessibility expert to hire. Depending on the size of the company, and the amount of digital information it produces, you may or may not want to hire a permanent accessibility person.

Finding a reputable auditing service can also be a challenge. With the growing public awareness of accessibility issues, there are a growing number of so-called accessibility experts popping up, taking advantage of the market for these services that has emerged with this awareness. You want to evaluate these auditor services to ensure their reputability.

Factors you might take into consideration when selecting an accessibility service could include:

- The number of years the service has been in business (the longer the better)
- The clients they have served (potential references)
- The accessibility of the service's website (dead giveaway to search elsewhere, if their site is not accessible)
- Whether their process aligns with accessibility auditing best practices (not required, but advisable)
- Whether they provide self-service tools (most good firms provide automated test tools)
- Whether accessibility auditing is their primary business (be wary of firms offering accessibility auditing as an add-on service for an unrelated primary business)
- Whether they offer training (the ability to train your staff is a good sign)

There are a number of reputable international services, so companies do not necessarily need to choose a local auditor. Since most accessibility regulations are based on WCAG, most international and local services audit based on those guidelines (or they should).

Self-Assessing

While searching for an accessibility-auditing firm on the Web, you come across a few accessibility-testing tools. Before you decide whether you need a third-party accessibility auditing service, you want to understand what you can do yourself with these tools to get a general sense of your company's accessibility status. You decide to do a little research on tools that can be used to test/check accessibility. You find there are a wide variety of free and commercial accessibility-testing tools.

AUTOMATED ACCESSIBILITY CHECKERS

There are quite a number of automated tools for testing web accessibility with varying degrees of coverage and accuracy. Much like choosing an accessibility auditor, choosing a good testing tool also requires a little critical evaluation. You may refer to existing evaluations of these tools and choose based on your needs. You may also want to adopt a number of accessibility checkers that complement each other.

> **Try This:** Copy the URL of your organization's website and paste it into the AChecker Web Accessibility Checker to see how accessible your website is.

Keep in mind that no automated accessibility checker can identify all potential barriers. In most cases, some human decision-making is required, particularly where meaning is being assessed. For example, does an image's text alternative describe an image accurately, or does link text effectively describe the destination of the link? Both require a human decision on the meaningfulness of the text.

> **Key Point:** Automated accessibility-testing tools cannot identify all potential barriers. A human must also be involved in testing, making decisions where meaning is being assessed.

There a number of different types of web accessibility checkers. Depending on your needs, one type may serve your organization better than others.

API-BASED ACCESSIBILITY CHECKERS

API stands for application programming interface. An API allows developers to integrate the accessibility checker into other web-based applications, such as web-content editors, to provide accessibility testing from within the application. For instance, with a content editor, the checker assesses the contents of the editor while creating and editing content. Tenon and AChecker provide APIs that can be used for integrations with other applications. To take advantage of an API, a developer would need to create the integration in many cases, though some applications may already have an integration with an accessibility checker.

TEXT-BASED ACCESSIBILITY CHECKERS

Text-based checkers typically output a list of accessibility issues it has identified; and, in some cases, provide recommendations to correct those issues. Some checkers may also categorize issues based on their importance or whether an issue is either a definite barrier or a potential barrier, which would need to be confirmed by a person. Some checkers evaluate single pages while others spider through a site and produce a site-wide accessibility report. These checkers often ingest one of the following: a URL of a web page, a user-uploaded HTML file, or copied and pasted HTML code; then, they produce a report based on the input provided. AChecker is a good example of a text-based accessibility checker, which also provides an API for integrations.

VISUAL ACCESSIBILITY CHECKERS

A third type of accessibility checker provides a visual presentation of a web page, pointing out where the issues appear on a page. The WAVE accessibility checker is a good example of a visual accessibility checker.

BROWSER PLUGIN ACCESSIBILITY CHECKERS

Some accessibility checkers are available as a browser plugin, making it easy, while viewing a web page, to click a button and get an accessibility report. The WAVE Chrome Extension is a good example of a browser-based plugin.

> **Toolkit:** Add an automated web accessibility checker such as AChecker or WAVE accessibility checker to your toolkit. They can be used to get a sense of the accessibility of your organization's website.

OTHER ACCESSIBILITY CHECKERS

The accessibility checkers mentioned above are just a tiny sample of the tools available. A well-crafted Google search, using terms like "accessibility checker" turns up many more. Or, you can browse through the list of accessibility checkers compiled by the W3C at the following link.

> **Readings & References:** Web Accessibility Evaluation Tools List

Other Types of Automated Testing Tools

While using automated web-accessibility checkers is a good start for assessing the accessibility of an organization's web resources, there are likely other tools needed to assess different types of content. Examples of such tools include:

- Colour Contrast Checkers
- Text Readability Testers
- HTML Markup Validation Testers
- PDF Accessibility Checkers

Manual Testing

As mentioned above, automated testing cannot identify all potential accessibility barriers. There are a few easy manual tests that can be used to identify issues automated checkers may not pick up.

- **Tab Key Test**: Determines whether all functional elements in web content are keyboard accessible. Place a mouse cursor in the location field of your web browser, then repeatedly press the Tab key on your keyboard and follow the cursor's path through the web page. Any functional elements like links, buttons, tabs, or forms, among others, should all receive focus while tabbing through the page and, while in focus, should operate by pressing the Enter key or spacebar.
- **Select-All Test**: Determines keyboard accessibility also. While your mouse cursor is focused on a web page, press CTRL+A (CMD+A on Macs) to select all the content on the page. Any items that are not selected are potentially not

keyboard accessible.

- **Screen Reader Testing**: A little more involved than the two tests above. Install a screen reader and navigate through a web page using the Tab key or arrow keys (in most cases). While listening to the output of the screen reader, determine if the output make sense; if not, there could be accessibility and usability problems. We recommend that web developers have a screen reader installed to test web content before it goes public. The ChromeVox screen reader works well for this purpose, installing as an extension for the Chrome web browser.
- **User Testing**: Though not always required, having actual users with disabilities navigate your company's web content can turn up a variety of usability issues that an accessibility expert may not identify. When recruiting people with disabilities for testing, ensure they are comfortable navigating the Web and are able to use their assistive technologies effectively to get meaningful feedback on usability issues. Novice assistive-technology users may encounter problems related to their inexperience, rather than problems with the accessibility of the content.

Toolkit: For full coverage of web accessibility auditing practices, consider enrolling your web developers in the Professional Web Accessibility Auditing Made Easy course.

Toolkit: The Accessible Information and Communication: A Guide for Small Business is another useful tool for accessing an organization's digital accessibility status.

Planning Possible Solutions

Understanding now that there are gaps in the company's compliance with accessibility guidelines, you start to think about the approaches you might take to implement solutions to fill those gaps.

Having spent some time learning about accessibility testing and trying the tools and strategies you came across, you discover there are lots of potential accessibility problems with the company's website. You share the results of your testing, and the tools and strategies with your senior web developer, who you ask to review and come up with an estimate of the time it would take to fix the issues you discovered.

The web developer reports back to you after a few days with a plan that will take longer than you expected. But, he also suggests, having reviewed the details of WCAG and the local accessibility regulations, perhaps he could prioritize the issues by first addressing the critical Level A issues described in WCAG, as well as addressing some of the easier Level AA issues.

He also suggests that you go back to the shopping cart vendor and see whether they are open to making some changes to their system to improve accessibility, reviewing the relevant business arguments if necessary in order to convince them the work will be good for their business.

Retrofitting versus Starting Over

Retrofitting an inaccessible website can be time consuming and expensive, particularly when the changes need to be made by someone other than the website's original developer. Adding accessibility to a new development project will require much less effort and expense, assuming the developers have accessibility forefront in their mind while development is taking place.

Sometimes retrofitting is the only solution available. For instance, a company is not prepared to replace its website with a new one. In such cases, it may be necessary to prioritize what gets fixed first and what can be resolved later. WCAG can help with this prioritizing. It categorizes accessibility guidelines by their relative impact on users with disabilities, ranging from Level A (serious problems) to Level AAA (relatively minor usability problems). These levels are described below.

- **Level A**: These issues **must** be resolved, or they will produce barriers that prevent some groups of people from accessing content.
- **Level AA**: These issues **should** be resolved, or they will create barriers that are difficult to get around for some groups of users.
- **Level AAA**: These issues **could** be resolved to improve usability for a wide range of people, including those without disabilities.

Level AA is the generally agreed-upon level most organizations should aim to meet, while addressing any Level AAA requirements that can be resolved with minimal effort. For organizations that directly serve people with disabilities, they may want to address more Level AAA issues, though it should be noted that full compliance with Level AAA requirements is generally unattainable, and in some cases undesirable. For instance, the WCAG lower-level high school reading level requirement is a Level AAA requirement. For a site that caters to lawyers, or perhaps engineers, high school-level language may be inappropriate, or even impossible, thus it would be undesirable to meet this guideline in such a case.

> **Key Point:** Level AA is the generally agreed upon level of accessibility most organizations should strive to meet. Where feasible, some Level AAA issues could also be addressed.

Working with Vendors and Developers

It is not uncommon for vendors, particularly those from jurisdictions that have minimal or no accessibility requirements, to resist an organization's requests to improve accessibility of their products. But, there are also vendors who will jump at an opportunity to take advantage of an organization's accessibility expertise to improve their product. The latter mentality is becoming more and more common as accessibility awareness grows around the world.

> You realize that replacing the shopping cart on the company's website, which was the subject of the complaint the company received, is not currently an option. The company has just renewed a three-year contract with the shopping cart provider and breaking that contract would be very costly. You understand that local regulations allow "undue hardship" as a legitimate argument for not implementing accessibility, and the company's lawyer agrees.
>
> Regardless, you also understand that your company is losing a potentially large number of customers, who leave the website and shop elsewhere when they encounter accessibility barriers. You want to demonstrate that the company takes accessibility complaints seriously, so you approach the shopping cart vendor with a proposal to help them improve the accessibility of their product.

Depending on the vendor, various approaches may be taken to either guide the vendor through the process of addressing accessibility in their products, or convince a vendor that this is something they need to do.

Ideally, you want the collaboration with a vendor to be a collegial one, where both your company and the vendor are benefiting. You could offer to have an accessibility audit performed on the software being (or having been) purchased, which should have been done anyway as part of the procurement process, and offer that audit to the company. Contributing to a vendor in this way may create a sense of "owing your company" and they will be more receptive to working together to address accessibility issues. When purchasing a new product, it is often possible to have the vendor cover the cost of an accessibility audit performed by an auditor of the company's choice. After the fact though, it's unlikely a vendor will want to take on that expense. Thus, an audit may be more of an offering to keep the vendor on the side of the company when asking for work from them that will likely be unpaid.

On the other hand, if a vendor is resistant, and not interested in your offer, as a last resort you may need to apply more cunning tactics, for instance, by threatening to publish the accessibility audit.

Of course, these scenarios describe only a couple potential vendor/client relationships, which really require a clear understanding of a vendor's position before approaching them with work they will likely not be paid for. Often the business arguments, introduced earlier, work well to convince vendors that accessibility is something that they can benefit from.

The bottom line is that some vendors will be more approachable than others and different strategies may be needed to have your accessibility requirements met by what may be considerable effort on the part of the vendor.

Suggested Viewing:

Video: Integrating Accessibility and Design: Five Hot Tips for Start-ups (Jutta Treviranus)

A YouTube element has been excluded from this version of the text. You can view it online here: https://pressbooks.library.ryerson.ca/dabp/?p=692

Video: An Introduction to Digital Accessibility

A YouTube element has been excluded from this version of the text. You can view it online here: https://pressbooks.library.ryerson.ca/dabp/?p=692

Developing a Company-Wide Strategy

The initial goals reached by the accessibility committee through its first few meetings are to create an "accessibility culture" where the whole company is aware of the importance of accessibility, creating a policy that guides how digital accessibility is addressed throughout the company.

With a number of gaps identified, the committee suggests several initial areas to focus on, which together will provide the basis for the company's accessibility policy.

1. Build awareness
2. Provide training
3. Communicate accessibility guidelines
4. Monitor adherence to guidelines (quality assurance)
5. Ensure accessible procurement practices

Building Awareness

One of the main reasons barriers arise is a lack of awareness. Most people have never met a person who is blind, let alone get to know such a person. As a result, they have little reason to think about accessibility and the potential barriers that may prevent a blind person from accessing digital content.

HIRING PEOPLE WITH DISABILITIES

One sure way to raise awareness of accessibility is to hire people with a disability. Having people with disabilities in a company's workforce helps build diversity, spread tolerance, and raise awareness of inequalities that are created when people have little or no experience with disability.

Hiring a person who is blind, for instance, will help expose your workforce to the challenges a blind person faces in everyday life and at work. This person could be a member of the accessibility committee, providing valuable input based on firsthand experience. This person could also provide screen reader testing of the company's digital resources and quickly identify accessibility issues before they become complaints.

People who are blind can be just as skilled at many activities as people who can see. There are blind programmers, accountants, teachers, lawyers, even hairstylists, to name just a few occupations. Many are highly educated with advanced degrees and doctorates.

Blindness is used here as an example because this group tends to face the most barriers in digital content. However, many people with disabilities are skilled workers. They are often overlooked as a result of systemic misconception of what people with disabilities are capable of.

RUN AN ACCESSIBILITY AWARENESS CAMPAIGN

Accessibility awareness campaigns can take a variety of forms and can involve publicity, training opportunities, presentations, an archive of resource materials, and an initiative for more company staff. Depending on the size and type of business, some of the following strategies could be used to implement an awareness campaign:

Posters

Posters can be placed in prominent places where staff are likely to encounter them. Some of these locations may include elevators, printer and copier rooms, lunch rooms, reception areas, and bathrooms. Posters could also be made available through an archive linked from the company's website, where accessibility resources are gathered.

Here is a sample of the types of posters that might be used in an accessibility awareness campaign: Accessible PDFs [PDF]

How-To Instructions

Instructional materials can also be created or gathered and added to the accessibility resources. Here are a few examples of the types of instructional materials that could be distributed:

- Creating Accessible Word 2010 Documents v 1.0 [PDF]
- Converting Word to Accessible PDF [PDF]
- 10 Key Guidelines [PDF]

Instructional Videos

Instructional videos can also be created, or gathered, and made available to staff. There are a great many videos from sources like YouTube that can be gathered into a single, easily accessible location, then publicized throughout the organization. Here are some examples of accessibility-related instructional videos. Search YouTube for more.

- Check Colour Contrast
- Automated Accessibility Checking
- HTML Validation
- Testing Accessibility with ChromeVox
- Creating an accessible PDF with Adobe Acrobat Pro 11

Email Campaigns

Email campaigns can also be another effective way to raise awareness, perhaps as part of a company newsletter include an "Accessibility Awareness" section. This section might include a link to video tutorials, perhaps updated from accessibility efforts ongoing throughout the company, links to various resources, or announcements about upcoming accessibility workshops. The possibilities are many, and, because a newsletter is distributed regularly, staff are consistently reminded of their accessibility responsibilities.

Or, you could set up a company mailing list, that anyone with an accessibility question can post to, as well as posting accessibility-related information similar to a newsletter. A person or two from the company's accessibility committee could be assigned to monitor the mailing list and provide responses when others have not replied. All employees can be added to the mailing list, so everyone becomes aware of ongoing accessibility efforts, and receive regular "reminders" through the dialog occurring there.

Workshops Presentations

Educating staff and teaching them new accessibility-related skills can help raise awareness throughout an organization. You may make workshops mandatory for particular staff, like web developers, or optional with a little bribery, like a pizza lunch, to get staff in the same room for a presentation and a question-and-answer session.

- Professional Web Accessibility Auditing Made Easy (free MOOC for developers)
- WAI-ARIA Workshop
- Accessible Documents Workshop
- Accessibility Testing with ChromeVox

Accessibility Knowledge Base

Providing an on-demand collection of resources related to accessibility and encouraging employees to use them can also help raise awareness. A knowledge base can be created with various types of educational materials, such as printable how-to tutorials, video, and examples of good practices. Employees should be encouraged to use these resources and contribute their own accessibility solutions. New additions to the knowledge base, or simply reminders to use what's there, can be encouraged through the company newsletter, or perhaps with a prominent link on the company's employee portal.

Workshops and Training Opportunities

Your accessibility resources are beginning to accumulate. You've decided to put up a few posters and add an accessibility awareness section to your company's monthly newsletter.

One of the things you'd like to do is develop a number of short workshops for staff in specific roles. Since your company distributes many PDF documents, you think this would be a good starting place for developing the workshops. However, you are not an expert in creating accessible PDF documents, so you will need to educate yourself first. You check with the web accessibility auditing firm you communicated with before doing your own informal audit of the company's website, and it turns out they offer an accessible documents workshop.

You also realize that the company's web developers need to be trained as well. While you could give your developers access to the resources you gathered on developing accessible websites, having an expert coach your developers will be a more effective way to get them trained quickly, and it will also give them the opportunity to ask questions, including ones specific to the company's website and the development processes in place at the company.

You plan to attend the workshops yourself, keeping an eye open for participants with a particular talent or enthusiasm for the topics being taught, thinking ahead to potential staff who could be recruited to the accessibility committee or to lead future workshops or presentations.

Training Efforts Can also Help Develop Awareness

There are a variety of topics related to accessibility that make good one- to three-hour workshops, which teach specific skills and knowledge or raise awareness of accessibility issues. During the early stages of developing digital accessibility business practices in an organization, it may be necessary to bring in an external service to provide training; however, over time, particular staff within the organization may be able to take on the role of instructor. The opportunity to teach topics further helps the trainer build expertise in the topic.

Here are a few suggestions that could be developed into workshops or lunchtime presentations:

ACCESSIBLE DOCUMENT AUTHORING

Audience: Office staff and others

Topics: Creating accessible Microsoft Word documents, converting Word documents to PDF, and using Adobe Acrobat Pro to make PDFs accessible

HOW PEOPLE WITH DISABILITIES USE THE WEB

Audience: Everyone

Topics: Meet a person who is blind, gain disability awareness, navigate the Web with a screen reader, review assistive technologies, and experience barriers firsthand

BASIC WEB ACCESSIBILITY

Audience: Web content authors and developers

Topics: Introducing the Web Content Accessibility Guidelines (WCAG), common accessibility barriers and their solutions, accessibility principles, and success criteria and techniques

ADVANCED WEB ACCESSIBILITY WITH WAI-ARIA

Audience: Web developers

Topics: Static vs. dynamic WAI-ARIA, JavaScript libraries, landmarks and roles, WAI-ARIA best practices

> **Toolkit:** For more advanced web interaction training for your organization's web developers have them review the ARIA Workshop.

WEB ACCESSIBILITY AUDITING

Audience: Web developers and web content authors

Topics: Automated testing, manual testing, screen reader testing, user testing, and types of audits and reports

> **Toolkit:** For more advanced training for your organization's web developers on accessibility auditing practices, enrol them in Professional Web Accessibility Auditing Made Easy.

MULTIMEDIA CAPTIONING

Audience: Web content developers, video production staff, everyone

Topics: Live versus asynchronous captions, open versus closed captions, Amara caption editor, YouTube captioning tools, captioning tools in other media authoring tools, captioning standards, captioning services, and described video

Self-Test 3

1. Which of the following factors might you take into consideration when selecting a service to audit the accessibility of your organization's website? Choose all that apply.
    1. How long the firm has been in business?
    2. Has auditing processes that align with the W3C accessibility auditing best practices.
    3. Provides automated self-assessment tools for accessibility checking
    4. Offers training for your staff.
    5. Auditing staff that have a university accessibility degree.
2. When self-assessing web accessibility, which of the following are strategies that might be used? Choose all that apply.
    1. Do a Tab key test.
    2. Use automated accessibility checkers.
    3. Have people with disabilities do testing
    4. Use a screen reader to navigate through a website.
    5. Do colour contrast testing using an online tool.

Answer Key to Challenge Test 3

An interactive or media element has been excluded from this version of the text. You can view it online here: https://pressbooks.library.ryerson.ca/dabp/?p=702

Accessibility Workshop Resources

Scan through the following workshop slides for an overview of the topics that would be included in training for web developers.

View on Prezi: Accessibility for Web Developers

An interactive or media element has been excluded from this version of the text. You can view it online here: https://pressbooks.library.ryerson.ca/dabp/?p=705

Toolkit: Add the Web Accessibility Workshop to your toolkit, and share it with your web developers

For more advanced training for web developers, that focuses on auditing practices and use of WAI-ARIA for making web interactivity accessible, review the topics of the following workshop.

View on Prezi: Accessibility Hands-on

An interactive or media element has been excluded from this version of the text. You can view it online here: https://pressbooks.library.ryerson.ca/dabp/?p=705

Toolkit: Add the Accessibility Hands-On Workshop to your toolkit, and share it with your web developers.

Developing Organization Accessibility Guidelines

To ensure consistency in the accessibility of the company's digital content, the accessibility committee has decided there needs to be a set of simple guidelines staff can follow. You start by creating three guidelines:

- Web Development Accessibility Guidelines
- Web Content Accessibility Guidelines
- PDF Accessibility Guidelines

Web Development Accessibility Guidelines

Though you could just have your developers review WCAG to understand what needs to be done to ensure the company's presence on the Web is accessible to everyone, there would be a great deal of "interpretation" required, and many aspects of WCAG that may not be relevant. Instead, you may want to identify the specific issues that need to be addressed in the company's websites, and develop a set of guidelines specific to those issues.

Use the 10 Key Guidelines [PDF] as your starting point. These guidelines can be distilled to create a brief list of issues developers must keep in mind when developing for the Web. These guidelines might be as follows, though depending on the organization, may require minor adapting to fit its needs. They should be easy to learn and memorize.

1. All images must have an alt attribute that describes the meaningful elements of the image, or the alt attribute is left empty if the image is decorative or otherwise meaningless.
2. All multimedia content with meaningful dialogue must have captions (video) or a transcript (audio).
3. Content with meaningful sections or topics must be structured using properly sequenced HTML headings.
4. If a series of items looks like a list, use proper list markup to format those items.
5. Where data is being presented in a table, the first row (and sometimes the first column) should be formatted as proper table header cells (i.e., <th>).
6. Ensure that when navigating through web content using the Tab key, the cursor moves from left to right, top to bottom, and does not veer from that pattern.
7. Ensure that the cursor's focus is easily visible when navigating through elements of the page with the Tab key.
8. When using colour to represent meaning, ensure that something other than colour also represents that meaning.
9. Ensure that contrast between foreground (text) colours and background colours provide sufficient contrast, at a ratio of 4.5:1 minimum for smaller text, 3:1 for larger text.
10. Ensure that all features that operate with a mouse, also operate with a key press.
11. Provide ways to skip past repetitive content using bypass links and ARIA landmarks.
12. Ensure that link text describes what would be found if the link were followed.
13. Ensure that accessible error or success feedback is provided after completing an action such as submitting a form or logging in, typically using the ARIA alert role with the element containing the feedback.
14. Ensure that all form fields are explicitly labelled using the HTML Label element.
15. Ensure that all functional elements whose operation is not immediately obvious, includes instructions on how to use them.

16. Describe the accessibility features of an application or website, and position a link to those details in the interface that will be easy to find for assistive technology users.

Web Content Accessibility Guidelines

The Web content accessibility guidelines will be very similar to those for web development listed above, though differing in that content typically tends to be less interactive than a user interface. As such, these guidelines focus more on the accessibility aspects of content.

1. All images must have an alt attribute that describes the meaningful elements of the image, or the alt attribute is left empty if the image is decorative or otherwise meaningless.
2. If images cannot be effectively described in alt text of 125 characters or less, provide a full description in the surrounding text, with a short description and a reference to the full description in the alt text.
3. Avoid using images of text, and where unavoidable, reproduce the meaningful text of the image as actual text in the image's surroundings.
4. All multimedia with meaningful dialogue must have captions (video) or a transcript (audio).
5. Content with meaningful sections or topics must be structured using properly sequenced HTML headings.
6. If a series of items looks like a list, use proper list markup to format those items.
7. When using colour to represent meaning, ensure that something other than colour also represents that meaning.
8. Ensure that contrast between foreground (text) colours and background colours provide sufficient contrast, at a ratio of 4.5:1 minimum for smaller text, 3:1 for larger text.
9. Where data is being presented in a table, the first row (and sometimes the first column) should be formatted as proper table header cells (i.e., <th>).
10. Ensure that all form fields are explicitly labelled using the HTML Label element.

PDF Accessibility Guidelines

PDF accessibility guidelines are similar to web content accessibility guidelines, though there are PDF specific requirements such as reading order, reading language, and document tagging that also need to be addressed to create an accessible PDF. Documents are typically created with Microsoft Word, saved as a PDF, then opened in Adobe Acrobat Pro to adjust the document's accessibility.

1. When creating a Word document to be converted to PDF, use proper headings to organize sections/topics in the document.
2. When creating a Word document to be converted to PDF, ensure all images have alt text describing the meaningful elements of the image.
3. When creating a Word document to be converted to PDF, ensure that any document with data tables have the "Repeat as header row at the top of each page" option checked in the table properties.
4. Use the Windows version of Word 2010+ to save Word documents as PDF with the "Document structure tags for accessibility" option checked when saving. (This is not supported on Macs.)
5. Use the Make Accessible tools of the Action Wizard in Adobe Acrobat Pro 11+ or Acrobat Pro DC to assess the accessibility of the converted Word document, and make accessibility adjustments.
6. Use the Reading Order tool in the Acrobat Pro toolbar on the left to arrange the elements in the PDF in a logical reading order.

Readings & References: Create and verify PDF accessibility (Acrobat Pro)

Monitoring Adherence to Guidelines

The company's web developers are working hard to educate themselves about web accessibility, and they are actively attending workshops and investigating accessible web development practices. You see improved accessibility in the company's websites, though there is still uncertainty about whether the sites comply with local accessibility requirements.

You return to the accessibility auditing firm you are currently in contact with while you have been developing the company's accessibility plan, and you ask for their assistance in auditing a number of new features that have been added to the main website. Ultimately though, you want to have an expert accessibility person on staff, who can provide accessibility audits on demand.

Web Content Quality Assurance

In an ideal situation, an organization's web developers would provide web accessibility audits. However, even with accessibility experience, it is wise to have a second pair of eyes review the work of the implementer. This task can be assigned to another developer or perhaps the Accessibility Champion. This is a typical practice in many development activities, and should be no different when accessibility is the subject. In the early stages of building accessibility knowledge into a company's culture, however, the expertise may not exist in-house to provide effective quality assurance, so third parties may need to be brought in.

Your senior web developer does have some experience with web accessibility, though he does not consider himself an expert. The other developers on staff are still new to the subject. As a result, there is not a sufficiently knowledgeable developer on staff to review the accessibility work of the senior member of the team. You decide that while your developers are building their accessibility expertise, you will bring in a third-party auditor, both to review and to train your developers.

> **Key Point:** Third-party auditing services can be a good source of expertise for managing accessibility quality assurance and training staff.

Accessibility reviews from an expert third-party auditor can act as a form of training. Typically, web accessibility reports will identify barriers, explain why particular barriers are a problem, and provide potential solutions to correct problems. They are typically written for a developer audience, so they are effective tools to educate developers. There will often be questions and feedback between the developer and the auditor, much like a student to teacher relationship. It may only take a few audit scenarios to bring developers to a point where they can do their own audits.

Examples of accessibility auditing services:

- WebSavvy Accessibility Consulting
- Deque Systems Inc.

- The Paciello Group
- Level Access

Automated Tools to Monitor Web Accessibility

Another option to help ensure the accessibility of an organization's web content is to implement an accessibility-monitoring system that will send alerts when potential problems are detected. There are a number of these systems available of varying cost and coverage, some of which include other quality assurance tests, like spell checking, finding broken links, testing text readability, and, even, PDF testing. Though these tools can be helpful in catching issues, they should not be relied upon exclusively to identify all potential accessibility issues that may arise in an organization's web content. Reviews by a human being should also be conducted on a regular basis. Reports could be shared through a knowledge base where all such reports and accessibility-related information can be stored.

Here are a few examples of accessibility monitoring applications that might be used to supplement accessibility quality assurance efforts of an organization.

Commercial systems:

- User1st
- Siteimprove
- Compliance Sheriff

Free open source

- Vamola (Italy) – now inactive, but a good base to build your own.

Document Quality Assurance

Document-accessibility auditing is relatively simple when compared with web accessibility auditing. Typically, a third-party review of documents is not necessary, though there may be cases where complex documents, like forms, do require more than basic skills to make them accessible.

For most documents, running the authoring software's accessibility review tool is sufficient to pick up any potential problems that may exist in a document. Training to use these tools can often be completed in a few hours, followed by opportunities to use these new skills to develop expertise. It may be helpful to have other document authoring staff quickly examine accessibility for the author, as a second review to ensure the document is as accessible as it can be. Having staff review others' work for accessibility can help strengthen accessibility awareness and maintain accessibility skills across a broader range of staff.

If you have a copy editor or production editor on staff, who reviews grammar, word usage, and spelling, and so on, this person may be a good candidate to develop expertise in document accessibility testing, to combine accessibility testing with copy editing.

Self-Test 4

1. When recommending accessibility requirements for web developers, it is best to send them directly to WCAG, on the W3C website.
   1. True
   2. False
2. When recommending guidelines for staff that produce PDF documents, WCAG should be suggested.
   1. True
   2. False

Answer Key to Challenge Test 4

An interactive or media element has been excluded from this version of the text. You can view it online here: https://pressbooks.library.ryerson.ca/dabp/?p=711

Other Digital Accessibility Considerations

Most of the digital accessibility concerns within your company revolve around the Web, electronic documents, and multimedia. In your research, you discover there are a few other areas where digital accessibility should be considered. These include branding, coding practice, and communication.

Branding

When considering branding elements for an organization, there are a few accessibility considerations to keep in mind.

Use of colour: Using the WCAG guidelines for colour use, ensure sufficient contrast between text colours, and the background colour they may appear over. At a minimum, use standard 10- to 12-point fonts and provide a contrast ratio of 4.5:1 or greater.

Try This: How to Test Colour Contrast.

Fonts: There are font characteristics that make fonts more or less legible, thus, more or less readable. "Fancy" fonts like Comic Sans for instance, can take longer to recognize, and this affects reading speed. This effect can be magnified for those with a print impairment.

Readings & References: Article on Font Legibility

Images with Text: While sometimes it is unavoidable, images of text should be used sparingly or avoided altogether. Text in images tends to degrade when magnified by those with low vision, making it difficult to read. For those who are blind and using a screen reader, text in images cannot be read at all. The text of a logo is an exception, but, if you also include a company motto as part of the logo, for instance, consider adding it as actual text next to the logo, rather than making it part of the logo image itself.

Coding

You might be surprised to know that there are quite a few blind or low-vision computer programmers. The way they code is much like any other coder does. Though code itself is not typically accessible or inaccessible. Good coding practices, such as effective use of space and effective commenting, can make code more usable for both sighted and blind coders.

Readings & References: How blind coders code

Communication

Many of the guidelines for creating accessible web content and documents also apply to communication. Where paper **documents** are distributed, be sure an electronic version is also available, making sure headings are properly used to structure topics, and describe in text form any visual elements in the communication.

Email can also be a major form of communication, both for promotional purposes and for personal communications. Emails can be created as plain text, rich text, or HTML. While plain text will generally be accessible, it can lack structural elements, which may be important for longer emails. Rich text and HTML can be marked up with headings, lists, alt text for images, and so on, to make them more accessible. Although there may be readers who display emails as plain text, in which case these formatted emails can be difficult to understand. For a typical personal email communication, plain text is usually fine. Where formatted text is used, it is advisable to also provide a plain text version as a fallback.

For more about accessible email, see the following optional readings.

Readings & References:

- Creating Accessible Emails
- Why send accessible email?

Text chat is also becoming a more common form of communication, often used by customers to contact support services through a real-time chat application linked from a website. These applications can often be inaccessible to blind users if they have not been developed with consideration for accessibility. The primary considerations when choosing a synchronous web-based chat application include:

- Properly implemented WAI-ARIA Live Region support
- Ability to pause new messages
- Access to a log of chat messages
- Keyboard access throughout the application
- An audio indicator when new messages are posted
- A visual indicator when new messages are posted
- Easy shortcut navigation between the message input field, the chat stream, and the connected users list (if applicable)

For more information on what makes a chat application accessible, as well as ratings for many popular chat applications (as of 2013), see the following Readings & References. Though the focus in the article is on chats used in education, it is relevant for other chat usage scenarios.

Readings & References: Are All Chats Suitable for Learning Purposes? A Study of the Required Characteristics

Service Equality versus Compliance

Though all services should ideally be accessible to anyone who attempts to access them, there may be occasions when it is just not possible to provide full access for everyone. Chats are one example where there may be unavoidable barriers, mainly because most of the available chat applications have room for accessibility improvements. That said, though, chat accessibility is improving.

Another good example of a technology that remains a challenge to access for some people with disabilities is videoconferencing systems. Though there have been efforts made by developers to improve the accessibility of these technologies, the currently available systems are generally difficult to use, are only partially usable, or are not usable at all with assistive technologies.

In cases such as these, all efforts should be made to procure the most accessible technology you can find, but with the understanding that they may not be accessible to everyone given the state of the art for these technologies. This is not to say organizations should not use them, but instead where they are used, acknowledgement should be provided about the limited access available, and provide an alternative where possible.

Similarly, primary service-delivery methods should be made accessible first, rather than resorting to providing alternative means of accessing these services for those with disabilities. For instance, do not create a website that is inaccessible because your organization wants to make use of some compelling, inaccessible technology, then create an alternative site for those accessing with assistive technology as a means of complying with regulated accessibility requirements. Despite best intentions, maintenance and upkeep of alternative sites are likely to fall behind that of the primary site. In general, the practice of providing alternative websites is frowned upon, except in cases where it is unavoidable because the technology being used is not yet available in an accessible form.

Managing the Impact of Change

You understand that there will be a significant change in the way the company does business, implementing what you see as a change in the culture of the company. Your employees already understand aspects of accessible customer service with the company's retail locations, such as ramps connecting floor levels within stores, elevators where stairs are used to move between levels, and checkout counters that accommodate wheelchair users, among other adjustments to "physical spaces." But, there is little knowledge within the company around issues of "digital accessibility."

Accommodation for accessibility of physical spaces is less likely to require change in the company's processes, but digital accessibility quite likely will. It will also involve changes in employee behaviour.

To counter any resistance to the changes that will be needed, you decide to educate yourself on change management. You gather all the information you need for forming arguments that you can use to convince your colleagues, leveraging the business arguments for implementing digital accessibility: these changes are something the company "wants to do" rather than "has to do," and these changes are good for the company.

So far you have experienced the "business case" for digital accessibility, and you have also been exposed to the legislative reasons behind it. Research suggests that companies who embrace a culture of accessibility are more successful/ profitable. However, acceptance of this culture isn't necessarily easy. One key issue you might experience in fostering a culture of accessibility is "resistance to change" from some of your employees/colleagues. They may wonder why dedicating resources (people, time, money) to implementing digital accessibility is important and how it will affect them.

Readings & References: Why Diversity Matters

People resist change for a number of reasons, most notably, due to fear of the unknown. Not knowing how the change will affect them directly (and to a smaller extent how it affects the company) will cause a number of employees to not readily or willingly accept (at least initially) the proposed changes. Linked with this is the fear of breaking routines, both in how people do their jobs and how it affects their life in general (hours, travel, and technology, etc.).

Resistance to change can occur when workers and management do not agree with the reasons for the change and the advantages and disadvantages of the change process.

Some reasons for resisting change include:

- Self-interest, which can occur when people are more concerned with the implication of the change for themselves rather than considering the effects for the company's success.
- Misunderstanding, because the purpose of the change has not been communicated effectively or has been interpreted differently.
- Low tolerance to change, because workers prefer having security and stability in their work.

Experience (and research) suggests that the best strategies for minimizing resistance to change is to communicate more effectively, to help people develop the skills/knowledge to handle the proposed changes, and to involve them in designing the changes to be implemented.

In this section of the unit, you will gain an understanding of some of the reasons why people may resist change which you may encounter in your organization and how to overcome them.

Change is difficult. The more prepared you are to deal with resistance, the better your chances for success in implementing the changes required. Watch this video outlining seven key strategies for overcoming resistance:

Video: 7 Strategies for Overcoming Resistance to Change

A YouTube element has been excluded from this version of the text. You can view it online here: https://pressbooks.library.ryerson.ca/dabp/?p=715

The seven strategies for overcoming change in the workplace follow below:

1. Structure the team to maximize its potential.
2. Set challenging, achievable, and engaging targets.
3. Resolve conflicts quickly and effectively.
4. Show passion.
5. Be persuasive.
6. Empower innovation and creativity.
7. Remain positive and supportive.

Readings & References:

- The Top 12 Typical Reasons for Resistance to Change
- Taxis vs Uber: A Perfect Example of Resistance to Change

Managing Change: Kotter's Model

Source: Andrews McMeel Syndication

Instilling digital accessibility culture throughout an organization is likely going to involve change, change that may meet with some resistance. Change can be uncomfortable, and for processes and practices that are ingrained in an organization over many years, it can be very difficult to upset this "status quo."

Depending on the scope of changes that must occur, preparing for change may be critical to successfully implementing a digital accessibility plan. It is helpful to have a framework from which to manage the changes that will occur as digital accessibility is being implemented throughout an organization.

But which model or framework should you use to help implement a successful accessibility plan? Change management books will introduce you to many models that may fit with your company culture and work processes. To give you a couple of samples of proven change models, we will use Kotter's eight-step model in this section and Lewin's three-step change model in the next. Both have many loyal followers and can help you think about how to start moving towards your new digital accessibility plan. Whichever model works best for you, it is important to remember that all of the steps must be followed in order for the model to be effective.

Kotter's Eight-Step Model for Leading Change

Dr. John F. Kotter at the Harvard Business School, devised the "Eight-Step Process for Leading Change." It consists of eight stages:

1. Create Urgency
2. Form a Powerful Coalition
3. Create a Vision for Change
4. Communicate the Vision
5. Remove Obstacles
6. Create Short-Term Wins
7. Build on the Change
8. Anchor the Changes in Corporate Culture

Video: Implement Change Powerfully and Successfully With Kotter's Eight-Step Change Model

A YouTube element has been excluded from this version of the text. You can view it online here: https://pressbooks.library.ryerson.ca/dabp/?p=718

Using Kotter's process, you imagine the pieces of your growing plan fitting into his framework as a way to optimize the strategies and ensure that your hard work pays off for the company.

1. Create Urgency

The obvious element of urgency in your company's case is the complaint and the suggestion by the customer that legal action may be taken if the company does not show active movement toward resolving the accessibility issues with the online store.

In addition, you may also argue that the market of people with disabilities is a large one, and the company is currently missing out on a good portion of this market, even sending potential customers to the competition. There is an opportunity to capture a growing market of older people with disabilities, many of whom are baby boomers who have reached a stage in their lives where they are losing their sight or hearing, and may not be as mobile as they used to be.

Most of all you need buy-in from senior people in the company. The business arguments discussed in Unit 2, carefully crafted to highlight the benefits to the company, can go a long way to convincing those who will ultimately determine whether a shift in the business culture has a chance of success or not. In the case of the Sharp Clothing Company, the threat of a lawsuit is a strong motivator for senior management, though ideally other business arguments should help lead to change before it reaches the point of legal action.

2. Form a Powerful Coalition

The accessibility committee you have established fills this step of the process, gathering leaders and knowledgeable staff, including those who may need accessibility accommodations, from across the company. This group of people will help define acceptable practices for the company by its' actions.

3. Create a Vision for Change

Understanding that many people will resist change, they want/need to understand where the company is heading. Articulating a clear vision for the company as to how the company wants to be seen and recognized with respect to accessibility is key here. The accessibility committee's plan – including steps to build awareness, develop training, communicate guidelines, monitor accessibility quality assurance, adjust procurement processes, review hiring practice, and consolidate these in a digital accessibility policy for the company – meets the objectives of this step.

4. Communicate the Vision

Through the newsletter campaign, strategically placed posters, training opportunities, a series of guidelines tailored to particular roles, and the involvement of people from across the company, you will communicate the company's move towards creating an inclusive business. This does require a highly coordinated and planned communication strategy that must be consistently applied by the change team.

5. Remove Obstacles

You decide to make the accessibility committee meetings open, so anyone who wants to attend may do so. You also decide to setup a virtual "suggestion box," positioned prominently on the company's employee web portal. There employees are encouraged to suggest improvements or identify where accessibility issues occur. Since most employees like to have a say in how things get done, take time to give them the opportunity to try ideas that are in alignment with the vision and strategies.

6. Create Short-Term Wins

The accessibility committee has come up with the idea of highlighting accessibility accomplishments in the quarterly newsletter and on the company's main websites. Once per year, all the accessibility related projects or suggestions would be gathered for the whole company to vote upon, with the winner receiving a weekend for two at a local hotel and spa. The reason short term wins are important is that they not only make the participants feel good about accomplishing something, but it also then gives them the momentum to move onto the next step or phase. By having one large undefined project, employees may give up if they can't see the finish line ahead of them.

7. Build on the Change

Through the wins that have been gathered, the submitters or implementers of more significant ones are given an opportunity to show off their accomplishments. Presentations are recorded and posted to the employee portal for all to see. Links to the videos are included in the quarterly newsletter. Acknowledging the accomplishments and those responsible for them acts as an important feedback mechanism and form of appreciation from the change team.

8. Anchor the Changes in Corporate Culture

With much of the accessibility plan in place, your plan is to formalize all of these elements into a company Digital Accessibility Policy. Culture defines what is acceptable behaviour or not, and the goal here is to make sure that your policy becomes part of your company culture and what your company values.

Readings & References: For more about the Kotter change management strategies, visit the following resources:

- Kotter International
  Kotter's Eight-Step Change Model
  Kotter's Eight-Step Change Model Infographic

Self-Test 5

1. Lewin's change model includes eight key steps for managing change.
    1. True
    2. False
2. Of the following, which one is not a stage of the Kotter Model?
    1. Communicate the Vision
    2. Create Urgency
    3. Misunderstanding
    4. Create Short-Term Wins

Answer Key to Challenge Test 5

An interactive or media element has been excluded from this version of the text. You can view it online here: https://pressbooks.library.ryerson.ca/dabp/?p=720

Managing Change: Lewin's Model

Kurt Lewin developed a change model involving three steps: *unfreezing*, *changing*, and *refreezing*. The model represents a very simple and practical model for understanding the change process. For Lewin, the process of change entails creating the perception that a change is needed, then moving toward the new, desired level of behaviour and, finally, solidifying that new behaviour as the norm. The model is still widely used and serves as the basis for many modern change models.

Video: Lewin's Change Management Model: Kurt Lewin's Unfreeze-Change-Refreeze Theory

A YouTube element has been excluded from this version of the text. You can view it online here: https://pressbooks.library.ryerson.ca/dabp/?p=722

Unfreezing

In the initial phase of investigating digital accessibility, you have been building awareness through the creation of the accessibility committee, and you have been investigating what aspect of the company's processes and human resources need to be adjusted. Hanging posters in the lunch room, elevators, and bathrooms, and the accessibility section in the monthly newsletter is raising awareness across the company, ahead of the retraining that is being planned.

You have also been practicing strategies for convincing staff at various levels that accessibility is a good thing for everyone, particularly those in senior positions, so that they understand the business, social, and economic aspects of accessibility. You have prepared yourself for resistance to the changes coming as part of the company's move toward becoming an inclusive organization.

Changing

Based on your knowledge of the Sharp Clothing Company's workforce, you have a series of short workshops planned that will help staff in various positions learn about their responsibilities to produce accessible products and deliver accessible customer service and introduce them to the tools to help them accomplish these.

To help standardize the processes, the accessibility committee has developed the guidelines for web developers, web content developers, and document authors and producers, so it is clear what steps must be taken in order to ensure they are producing products and services that will be accessible to everyone. The training being planned uses these guidelines as a framework for instruction, with staff receiving hands-on experience with the tools and processes associated with their jobs , and they have a reference they can continue to use and refer to until they have mastered the tasks and strategies they were taught.

Refreezing

To ensure that attention to accessibility remains high, the company newsletter will continue to highlight particular accessibility accomplishments by staff, and present various accessibility tips and interesting bits of knowledge to keep awareness high.

The yearly contest for the best accessibility implementation will also help keep awareness high, publicizing ongoing efforts, and giving people throughout the company the opportunity to vote on who should receive the "Spa Weekend for Two."

The plan is to hire on a screen reader user to help with accessibility testing, to be a member of the accessibility committee, to work day-to-day with the staff at head office, and to help keep awareness high.

Having an employee who is blind will also help other staff members become accustomed to people with disabilities, and become more aware of barriers that may prevent some people from participating fully.

Try This: Knowing that most people will resist change for a variety of reasons, let's watch a brief clip from a popular TV show *Big Bang Theory* which demonstrates how some people react to change.

Video: **BigBang Theory – Comida china sin Howard (The Dumpling Paradox)**

A YouTube element has been excluded from this version of the text. You can view it online here: https://pressbooks.library.ryerson.ca/dabp/?p=722

Questions to think about:

- Have you ever encountered a situation similar to this? If so, how did you handle it?
- Do you often find yourself as the waiter, trying to offer suggestions to move things along? Were your ideas well received or implemented?
- What if you had to manage someone like Sheldon?

Identifying Forces For and Against Change

Reflecting back to the "Dumpling Paradox" video clip, here are some of their reasons for wanting to order dinner:

- They were hungry.
- They were familiar with this restaurant.
- They had past experience knowing what to order.

Yet, there were equally compelling arguments presented for not ordering their regular items:

- Needing to now order for three persons rather than four.
- Their regular menu choices would now lead to too much food to split three ways.
- Too much food overall for them to enjoy.

What we have just done is to conduct a **Force Field** analysis, a key process of the Kurt Lewin Change Model. It helps you identify the compelling reasons for change and those "forces" which will oppose change. This is a common first step many change leaders use to assess a situation before introducing something new. You can learn more about the process from Change Management Coach.

Force Field Exercise

As a personal exercise to understand a force field analysis, complete the columns below to identify the driving forces and restraining forces as to why you might consider joining a local gym. An example of how to identify the force field will be provided later in this section.

Force Field Example – Should I join a local gym?

Driving Forces	Restraining Forces

Activity: Responding to Resistance

When implementing organizational change, there will inevitably be those who resist or even outwardly oppose the need for change. From senior executives with considerable power and influence to those "working in the trenches," each person approaches change from their own perspective and will have different reasons for being concerned.

Readings & References: In the article Overcome The 5 Main Reasons People Resist Change, the author provides five main reasons people resist change:

- Fear of the unknown/surprise
- Mistrust
- Loss of job security/control
- Bad timing
- An individual's predisposition toward change

Change can be uncomfortable, and, in hopes of avoiding this discomfort, people will often present arguments against it. In this activity, you will consider what arguments your colleagues at Sharp Clothing might make in an attempt to stop or hinder your efforts to introduce accessibility compliance.

Write three possible arguments a resistant employee may give in opposition to implementing digital accessibility, and write a convincing counterargument for each that would help reduce resistance. In each, **indicate who the target employee is and/or their role within the organization**.

Hints: You might search the Web for statistics or other evidence that demonstrates the benefits of an accessible organization.

Here are some example arguments against change. You may use these or come up with others.

- This has been the way we have always done it.
- We have no people with disabilities as clients.
- It would cost too much to make our website accessible.
- A blind person would not be able to access our website.
- We don't have the time or resources to implement your accessibility plan.
- We can just use the auto-captioning on YouTube for our promo videos.
- The laws do not apply to us; we only have 25 employees.

Creating Digital Accessibility Culture: Takeaways

In this unit, you learned that:

- Accessibility auditing is an important step. Choosing a reputable service involves careful consideration focusing on key reputability factors.
- Two approaches to accessible websites are retrofitting and starting over. The correct approach for your situation will need to consider several factors including outsourcing the work to external vendors.
- Building a company-wide strategy about accessibility includes building awareness, hiring people with disabilities, focused presentations, and training.
- Web development accessibility guidelines focus on user interaction with a website, whereas *web content accessibility* guidelines focus more on standards compliance. Both are important.
- Several approaches should be used to monitor adherence to accessibility guidelines including unbiased quality assurance reviews and the use of automated tools.
- Implementing accessibility will include managing change. Kotter's Eight-Step Model for Leading Change and Lewin's Three-Step Model are two common models that can help plan and facilitate the implementation.
- Resistance by staff may be the most challenging element in implementing change. Overcoming the five main reasons people resist change needs to be part of your change management strategy.

5. PROCUREMENT AND ACCESSIBILITY POLICY

Procurement and Accessibility Policy

What brought about the decision to develop a culture of accessibility throughout the Sharp Clothing Company was the purchase of a shopping cart application for the company's website without considering and properly evaluating it for accessibility. You decide to investigate strategies for procuring accessible products and services, and you start looking at how accessibility procurement practices will fit into the digital accessibility policy you have been piecing together.

This unit will provide you with guidance on how to create a context for accessible procurement practices through a broader accessibility policy. It will also provide information on how to document your company's accessibility requirements when communicating with external vendors, and how to assess and work with vendors to support accessibility for all users.

Objectives and Activities

Objectives

By the end of this unit, you should be able to:

- Explain the elements that make up an accessibility policy.
- Explain key differences in procuring and contracting for accessibility.
- Create an accessibility statement focusing on inclusion.
- Describe strategies for assessing a vendor's accessibility knowledge.
- Critique and validate vendor accessibility claims against recognized standards.

Activities

- Critique Accessibility Claims

Digital Accessibility Policy

The pieces of the Digital Accessibility Policy are coming together. You understand that procurement also needs to be included as part of the policy. Before proceeding, you decide to take a look at what others have done in creating procedures for developing such a policy. You also want to look at policies others have published. You discover a wide range of policies, from simple statements outlining an organization's commitment to web accessibility, to complex documents that describe in great detail each aspect of an organization's digital accessibility requirements.

Some policies focus specifically on the Web, ensuring web content is accessible to everyone. Others are more general, covering a wide range of accessibility matters including customer service standards as well as accessibility of the built environment.

You decide that your focus will remain on developing a policy that encompasses digital accessibility, which includes web content, documents, multimedia, and information technology (IT).

Creating a Web Accessibility Policy

WebAIM, at the Center for Persons with Disabilities at Utah State University, undertook a project to develop an Eight-Step Implementation Model for creating an organization's web accessibility policy, recognizing that implementing and maintaining a policy is a cultural or systemic issue within that organization. It needs to be ingrained at all levels to be successful and continue as business practice, with all employees committed to an inclusive presence on the Web.

WebAIM describes the steps as follows:

1. **Gather Baseline Information:** This step is essentially an audit of the organization's website(s) current accessibility status.
2. **Gain Top-Level Support:** In order for an accessibility policy to work, it needs buy-in from the top levels of the organization.
3. **Organize a Web Accessibility Committee:** Assemble stakeholders from various groups in the organization, including respected individuals from these groups, web development staff, and where possible, people with disabilities.
4. **Define a Standard:** Create an organizational web accessibility standard, which could be based on WCAG 2.0 with adjustments to match organizational needs.
5. **Create an Implementation Plan:** Set timelines and priorities, delegate responsibilities, and monitor progress.
6. **Provide Training and Technical Support:** Identify those who publish to the Web, assess their skills, plan training for different groups, create lists of resources, tools, code samples, and manuals that provide guidance on producing accessible web content.
7. **Monitor Conformance:** Schedule annual/semi-annual website reviews, define "monitoring" in someone's job description, and ensure that person is well versed in HTML authoring and web accessibility.
8. **Remain Flexible:** Plan for change, such as changes in staff, standards, and technologies.

Readings & References: For a full description of each of these steps, see the Eight-Step Implementation Model.

Examples of Web Accessibility Policies

The following are a few good examples of web accessibility policies from different types of companies and organizations around the world. Scan through them to get a sense of the variability that exists in the types of information included in these policies.

Readings & References:

FOOD DRINK ENTERTAINMENT

Starbucks Customer Service Policy (AODA)

GOVERNMENT

Accessibility Policy: How can I help?

Massachusetts State Treasury

European Union

UNIVERSITIES

Ohio State University Web Accessibility Policy and Standards (Section 508, ADA, WCAG)

CULTURAL ORGANIZATIONS

Musée d'art contemporain de Montréal Web Accessibility Policy

BANKS AND COMMERCE

Ontario Securities Commission

Procurement as Part of Digital Accessibility Policy

While the focus of this unit is on procuring accessible information technology (IT), accessible procurement in general should be part of a larger policy that addresses accessibility at the organizational level. A digital accessibility policy can also fall within a larger accessibility policy which addresses other aspects such as access to physical spaces and access to customer service.

Digital accessibility as a policy on its own will be introduced here to set the context for our discussion of procurement in this unit and the discussion of hiring practices in the next unit.

Video: Creating a Culture of Accessibility

A YouTube element has been excluded from this version of the text. You can view it online here: https://pressbooks.library.ryerson.ca/dabp/?p=736

Procurement in Accessibility Policy

Procuring accessible IT will affect numerous elements of an accessibility policy.

In the early stages of developing an accessibility policy, assessing the baseline accessibility level will include taking stock of third-party software used by the organization. These might include a content management system (CMS), a learning management system (LMS), point-of-sale systems, human resource management systems, and a variety of other types of systems for administering day-to-day operations. Each of these at some point would have gone through a procurement process.

Here are some examples of how procurement fits into an organization's overall digital accessibility policy:

- In order to implement accessible procurement requirements, agreement is needed from the organization's top level.
- When providing training and support, staff need to be taught how to use accessibility features within the systems procured.
- Ongoing monitoring is needed to ensure that upgrades to systems don't compromise accessibility. Often, when software as a service (SaaS) is being used, system updates behind the scenes go unnoticed by typical users of the system.

Readings & References: For more about procurement and accessibility policy, visit these resources:

- Ontario Public Service: Policies That Make Accessibility Work
- Accessibility Rules for Procurement (Ontario)

Ontario Integrated Accessibility Standards Regulation:

- A guide to developing an accessibility policy for organizations with 1-49 employees [PDF]
- Developing accessibility policies and a multi-year accessibility plan: A guide for organizations with 50 or more employees [PDF]

Additional Resources:

- Accessibility for Ontarians with Disabilities Act A Comprehensive Guide for Developing Accessibility Policies and Accessibility Plans [PDF]
- Let the Buyer be Aware: The Importance of Procurement in Accessibility Policy
- Developing Organizational Policies on Web Accessibility
- How to create an accessibility plan and policy

Procuring Accessible Information Technology

Many organizations will have in-house developers who create and maintain web content and who can be trained to implement web accessibility in their development practices. Most organizations however, will **purchase or license third-party software** or Web applications for particular purposes rather than having their in-house developers create them. It is generally more economical to license than it is to create complex systems like a content management system (CMS) or a customer relationship management system (CRMS).

The accessibility of these third party tools should always be assessed before committing to a particular system. This often starts by **asking vendors to describe the accessibility features** of their product in a request for proposals (RFP). This request might include:

- A checklist of desirable accessibility features that the vendor completes
- A request for a **Voluntary Product Accessibility Template (VPAT)** if the company is in the U.S.
- A request for a third party evaluation of the product being procured

Here are some tips to follow once you receive accessibility information from vendors:

1. **Do some research and take the time to carefully assess the vendor's claims for accuracy:** Because vendors are often in competition to win your business, it is possible that they may exaggerate claims, word claims to work around known issues in their products, and, in the worst cases, make false claims about the accessibility of their products. It can be helpful to look at the vendor's own website, test it with an automated checker, and look for accessibility information there. This can tell you a lot about the vendor's accessibility knowledge. Failing to assess a vendor's claims may have significant legal consequences, if accessibility claims are made against your organization and it can be shown that due diligence was not employed when acquiring a product.
2. **Think beyond "yes or no":** It is not uncommon to shortlist a product for purchase or licensing that is not fully accessibility compliant, but that does have a good variety of accessibility features. It can be counterproductive to make absolute compliance a requirement. You may find for some complex systems that there are no fully compliant offerings. A system may not be compliant, but it may be the most accessible of a class of systems. Aim to procure the system that provides the best mix of required features and accessibility.

Once your organization has decided on procuring a system, it is important to **build accessibility requirements into the contract**, so that if issues are later found that present significant barriers, vendors must take responsibility and provide solutions.

Some vendors will be receptive to accessibility requests, particularly those in regions where accessibility laws affect their ability to sell their products. It is not uncommon for vendors to have little knowledge of accessibility, having never had such a request (but who, when educated, may be very happy to accommodate those requests). To set yourself up for success, simply plan to **work with vendors that understand the importance of accessibility**.

Readings & References: For more about strategies for procuring accessible IT, review the following resources.

- The IT Procurement Toolkit (Ireland)

- Managing accessibility in the public procurement of ICT (EU)
- University of Washington: Procuring Accessible IT

Creating an Accessibility Statement

> While looking at accessibility policies developed by other organizations, you come across several websites that include an "accessibility statement." You decide such a statement would be a good addition to your company website. You spend some time reviewing statements others have posted to their sites, then you gather a list of elements to include in the statement you will create for your company.

An accessibility statement can be used on a website and in various documentation to let visitors and stakeholders know about the company's commitment to accessibility. Though an accessibility statement will help inform others of an organization's efforts and commitment, it is not a requirement for compliance.

Outlined below are several elements you may consider including in an accessibility statement. Once a statement has been prepared, it should be linked prominently on a website, preferably near the top of the site, where it will be easier to find for those who are navigating with assistive technology.

Statement of Commitment

A standard statement of commitment for both the website and the policy document can be created to guide an organization's accessibility efforts. The following is an example of what a statement of commitment might look like:

> At XYZ Company, we are committed to ensuring our goods and services are accessible to everyone and to removing barriers that may prevent some people from accessing these goods and services.

Statement of Compliance

If your website has been reviewed, either by an external auditor or one internal, you might choose to include a statement that describes the level of compliance the website meets. A statement of compliance must include **the date** the site was judged to be compliant. Because websites tend to change over time, compliance can only be claimed for the date on which an audit was completed. A copy of an audit report might also be linked from the statement, but is not required. A second element that must be included in the compliance statement is **the specification** or standard the site is claiming compliance with. In most cases, this will be WCAG 2.0. The final required element is the **level of compliance**, either Level A, Level AA, or Level AAA (if WCAG is the specification being used).

A simple statement of compliance might look like the following:

> On January 20, 2017, this website conformed with the Web Content Accessibility Guidelines 2.0 at Level AA.

A compliance statement may also include additional information about the scope of the claim. For example, the claim may only refer to a particular area of a website, in which case that portion should be described in the claim, such as "the publicly accessible areas of the site." Or, a statement may only apply to parts of the website the organization has control over, and not apply to third-party web applications or services that may be used. A statement, then, might include omissions, such as "not including the shopping cart application."

Known Accessibility Issues

It is not uncommon for an accessibility statement to acknowledge potential barriers that an organization may be aware of, that are perhaps a work in progress, or may refer to third-party tools or technology that may not be available in an accessible form. Though this statement should not be an excuse for using less-than-accessible tools or applications on a website, it can help alleviate complaints when an organization demonstrates their awareness and their plans to remedy barriers over time, or to make public their use of technology that may not have an available accessible alternative. One such example may be videoconferencing systems. Though these are often required tools for communication, there is no current videoconferencing system that would comply with accessibility requirements.

An example of a known-issues statement might look like the following:

> We are aware of a number of potential barriers in the Shopping Cart application that may prevent some users from purchasing products from our website. We are working with the vendor to address these issues, and we are looking at potential alternatives that may be implemented in the future. If you are experiencing difficulties using the shopping cart to make purchases, please contact our online support team at (111) 555-2134, who will be able to assist you with your purchase.

You may also include general contact information in the statement to allow site visitors to report any accessibility problems they may encounter.

Website Accessibility Features

Another element that might be included in an accessibility statement is a description of the accessibility features that have been implemented on a website. This can be helpful for users who need accessibility features, so they do not need to discover these features on their own, reducing the effort in learning how to use website features when using assistive technology.

Some of these features may include:

- Keystrokes for direct keyboard access to features
- Use of captions and/or transcripts with multimedia
- Use or WAI-ARIA to create interactive elements
- Use of navigation elements such as landmarks, bypass links, and headings
- Instructions for using complex features, like a photo gallery or shopping cart application
- Descriptions of a site layout

> **Readings & References:** Examples of accessibility statements:

- The Chang School's Accessibility Statement
- City of Brantford Web Accessibility Statement
- The University of Edinburgh Accessibility Statement

Readings & References: Nomensa: Writing an Accessibility Statement.

Toolkit: Accessibility Statement Generator

Self-Test 6

1. How many steps does the WebAIM accessibility policy implementation model have?
    1. 5
    2. 6
    3. 7
    4. 8
    5. 9
    6. 10
2. When creating an accessibility statement, which of the following were mentioned as elements that might be included in the statement? Choose all that apply.
    1. Known accessibility issues
    2. Website accessibility features
    3. Statement of commitment
    4. Statement of compliance
    5. The name of the website's developer

Answer Key to Challenge Test 6

An interactive or media element has been excluded from this version of the text. You can view it online here: https://pressbooks.library.ryerson.ca/dabp/?p=744

Stating Accessibility Requirements

There are a variety of circumstances where accessibility requirements may need to be explicitly stated, for example:

- Requests for proposals (RFP)
- Purchase contracts
- Purchasing procedures
- Design specifications

There may be other documents in an organization that also require accessibility statements or requirements, such as process documents or literature about the organization or its products. An organization's accessibility committee members may be asked to gather relevant documents from their respective areas within the organization in order to produce a full list of relevant document-accessibility statements. Here, we will look at RFPs, and the request for accessibility information they should contain.

Request for Proposals (RFP)

GENERAL ACCESSIBILITY STATEMENT

The National Center on Disability and Access to Education (NCDAE) provides a number of examples for wording that could be included in RFPs, for organizations in the U.S. (see Sample 1 below). We have provided an AODA-adapted version (see Sample 2 below). While statements such as these make relatively clear what the requirements are to a person knowledgeable in accessibility-related issues, they may not be explicit enough to produce a good description of the product's accessibility features. Such wording also uses absolute language such as "Applicants must state their level of compliance...." Given that many products may not fully comply, language such as this can be used as a starting point, but it should be supplemented with more specific requirements.

Sample 1: Contained in a Request for Proposal (Section 508)NOTICE – All electronic and information technology (EIT) procured through this RFP must meet the applicable accessibility standards of 36 CFR 1194. 36 CFR 1194 implements Section 508 of the Rehabilitation Act of 1973, as amended, and is viewable at the following URL: http://www.section508.gov The following Section 508 technical standards are applicable to this RFP, as a minimum: "Software Applications and Operating Systems (1194.21)", "Web-based Intranet and Internet Information and Applications (1194.22)", "Video or Multimedia Products (1194.24) C.4" Applicants must state their level of compliance to applicable sections to be considered for purchase under this RFP.

Sample 2: Contained in a Request for Proposal (AODA)NOTICE – All information and communication technology (ICT) procured through this RFP must meet the accessibility standards of the Integrated Accessibility Standards Regulations (IASR) Reg. 191/11, s. 14 and O. Reg. 191/11, s. 15. Regulation 191/11, s. 14 implements the Information and Communications Standards of the Accessibility for Ontarians with Disabilities Act (AODA), with regard to accessible websites and web content, and Regulation 191/11, s. 15 with regard to Educational and training resources and materials, viewable at the following URL: http://www.ontario.ca/laws/regulation/110191#BK15. The associated technical standards for these regulations are specified in the W3C's Web Content Accessibility Guidelines 2.0, viewable at the following URL: http://www.w3.org/TR/WCAG20/. Applicants must state their level of compliance to applicable sections to be considered for purchase under this RFP.

SPECIFIC ACCESSIBILITY REQUIREMENTS

Consider developing a specific list of accessibility requirements for vendors, using the WCAG 2.0 10 Key Guidelines introduced in Unit 2 as a starting point, as well as any other requirements your organization may deem necessary.

With this strategy in mind, we have created a sample checklist for vendors. The checklist is structured so that vendors can easily indicate their level of compliance with various requirements, and also provide explanations for the indicated state of compliance. These explanations are particularly important for items identified as "partially compliant."

Toolkit: Download the Sample Vendor Accessibility Compliance Checklist [PDF] and add it to your Toolkit. Depending on the type of product being procured, not all of the 10 Key Guidelines may be relevant. Adjust the list accordingly to specify only those features relevant to the product type being procured.

Assessing Vendor Knowledge of Accessibility

Assume that a vendor's proposal is accepted for review and competition and they are asked to provide a demonstration. It is at this point when you can move into more particular, perhaps technical, questions about specific accessibility features of their product.

Assessing a Vendor's Website

It is often easy to get a sense of a vendor's knowledge and commitment to accessibility by simply looking through their website.

- Sample a few pages and run them through an automated accessibility checker and HTML validator. How well do they do? The results will be a good indication of the quality and accessibility of work the company does.
- Does the vendor's website have a prominent **accessibility statement**? Though not a requirement, if they do have one, it's a good indication the company cares about accessibility.
- Does that statement, if there is one, have a compliance claim and **are accessibility features on the site listed**? If the accessibility features are listed, it likely means they are thinking about people with disabilities who are visiting their site, which is one step above thinking about accessibility in general.
- If there is a **demo of the software** you intend to procure, sample a few screens for checker and validator testing. How well do they do? You may be able to decide in this manner whether the software you are intending to procure from this company has the potential or not to meet the accessibility requirements of your organization.
- If an RFP is being issued, you may want to mention to vendors that their website may be reviewed for accessibility. Or, you may want to review websites prior to an RFP, to aid with shortlisting vendors to approach.

Self-Test 7

1. When vendors are describing the level of accessibility their product complies with, they should mention Level AAA.
    1. True
    2. False
2. If a vendor mentions a few known accessibility issues in their accessibility statement for a product, purchasing, or licensing the product should be avoided.
    1. True
    2. False

Answer Key to Challenge Test 7

An interactive or media element has been excluded from this version of the text. You can view it online here: https://pressbooks.library.ryerson.ca/dabp/?p=753

Accessibility Questions During Product Demonstrations

During a product demonstration, specific and technical questions should be asked. It is a good idea to have the responses from the RFP accessibility requirements in hand so they can be clarified.

In addition to clarifications in the proposal's accessibility responses here are some additional questions that can be asked to assess a vendor's level of accessibility understanding and their willingness to address accessibility issues in their software to meet your organization's requirements.

> **Toolkit:** See Accessibility Questions for Product Demonstrations for a collection of questions that can be asked while interviewing vendors.

Here is the list of 10 possible questions and expected answers:

1. Which accessibility standards does your product comply with? At which Level (if WCAG)?

Depending on the jurisdiction of the vendor, a local accessibility standard should be mentioned (e.g., Section 508 in the U.S.; AODA in Ontario), or mention WCAG. Added points if the vendor is from a different jurisdiction, and mentions the requirements of your jurisdiction, if different from their own.

At a minimum, where WCAG is the vendor's guideline of choice, Level A should be mentioned, or talk about what remains to be addressed to meet Level A. If Level AA is mentioned, added points could be given. If Level AAA is mentioned, that is a warning sign, since very few if any complex systems will meet Level AAA requirements. Ask what AAA features have been implemented in the system.

2. Is your product accessible without a mouse? Please demonstrate.

The answer should always be "Yes." The vendor should be able to demonstrate by using the Tab key to navigate through the user interface (UI). All functional elements, like menus, links, buttons, and forms, etc., should all be able to receive focus, and users should be able to navigate through menus and open elements using only the keyboard. Watch out for elements that can receive focus, but do not operate with a keypress.

3. Has your product been tested with assistive technologies? If so, with which ones?

Should answer "Yes."

Should mention a screen reader at a minimum. Should be able to identify which screen readers, such as ChromeVox, JAWS, NDVA, etc. Added points if they also mention Voiceover and/or Talkback for mobile devices.

4. Who did the testing?

The developers of the software should be mentioned. Screen reader testing should be part of the development process. Or, a particular accessibility person within the organization may be the tester. Added points if people with disabilities were used in testing, or a third party accessibility expert. Is the third party tester reputable, if one was used?

5. What was the testing methodology? What were the results?

Should mention a combination of automated and manual testing strategies, and screen reader testing. Added points if testing with people with disabilities is also part of their testing process.

Ideally mention the level of conformance reached, as well as acknowledging any issues that may remain, and what they plan to do to address those issues. Answering "fully accessible" is a warning sign. Very few systems will be fully accessible to everyone.

6. How is accessibility built into your company's quality assurance (QA) process?

Should talk about the development process at a minimum, and where accessibility design and testing tasks fit into the process. Added points if the vendor goes into detail about the Web accessibility policy implemented at the company.

7. If you roll out upgrades after we purchase the product, how can you assure us the upgrades will not break accessibility?

Should refer back to the QA process, local upgrade testing before pushing updates to production environments. Added points if third-party accessibility expert is involved.

8. Does your product make use of WAI-ARIA? If it does, how so?

Where a product has a fairly complex, interactive UI, the answer should be "Yes." This indicates the vendor understands the complex accessibility issues associated with custom-built web interactivity.

May mention using ARIA landmarks. Added points if the specific ARIA attributes are mentioned for particular types of interactions, for example, using menu-related ARIA for complex menu, tab panel-related ARIA for tab panel presentations, and so on. Perhaps mention libraries used to implement ARIA, like jQuery or MooTools, or perhaps a custom-made ARIA library created by the vendor.

9. Does your product adapt responsively to different screen sizes? Please demonstrate.

Should answer "Yes." Should be able to grab the corner of a browser window and drag it inward to reduce the window size, and the content should adapt cleanly as the window size increases and decreases. Should also be able to demonstrate the product on a mobile device like a smartphone or tablet, and have the UI adapt to the device's screen size.

10. Does your product magnify cleanly using just a browser's zoom feature? Please demonstrate.

Should answer "Yes." Should be able to use the browser's zoom function to increase the size of the content to at least 200% without the content flowing off the side of the screen or overlapping with adjacent content. Added points for zoom sizes greater than 200%. Good zoom adaptation indicates relative measures (em, %) have been used to size elements rather than absolute measures (px, pt), which is also a requirement for good responsive designs.

Voluntary Product Accessibility Template (VPAT)

A Voluntary Product Accessibility Template, or VPAT as it is commonly known, is a checklist that companies who supply the U.S. government can fill out to document the accessibility of their products. Because a VPAT is completed by the vendor, they have a tendency to present products in a better light than what may actually be the case. As a result, any time you are presented with a VPAT, it is important that a person knowledgeable in web accessibility critically reviews the document.

> **Toolkit:** Download the VPAT 2.1 [DOC] form and add a bookmark/favourite to your Tool Kit.

> **Readings & References:** VPAT 2.1 is now available.

The VPAT 2.1 Web and software accessibility requirements are based on WCAG 2.0. VPAT 2.1 also encompasses the European Union's EN 301 549 accessibility requirements, and the Revised Section 508 requirements of January 2017.

Getting a Second Opinion

Even expertly created audits or assessments can benefit from a second opinion. Not all auditors approach accessibility requirements the same way. Some may have a more strict approach, following guidelines and techniques more stringently. Others may have a more practical approach, taking into consideration a range of variables such as budget, human resources, and adaptive technology support for particular techniques, etc. Those with a practical approach come up with solutions that best fit the circumstance, perhaps foregoing some of the strict compliance rules in favour of feasibility.

Web Accessibility Auditing Services

There are a growing number of companies that provide professional web accessibility auditing services. Not all of these companies are reputable and may not have an expert understanding of web accessibility. Some of the same strategies one might use to evaluate the accessibility knowledge of a vendor can also be used to evaluate the knowledge of a potential auditor.

If you would like a third-party accessibility auditing service to evaluate a product your organization is intending to procure, here are a few things you should look for:

1. **Are the auditors web developers?** Many issues that present barriers are the result of using HTML, WAI-ARIA, or JavaScript incorrectly. A web developer (or a person with a strong understanding of these technologies) can accurately identify the origins of more complex issues and offer effective solutions.
2. **Does the service provide tools?** The more reputable services develop their own tools such as automated checkers, contrast evaluators, and browser plugins, etc. that the average user can use to test accessibility for themselves. A good collection of tools is a good indicator that the service knows what it is doing. Tools may also indicate that developers are on staff.
3. **How long has the service been in business?** If you can't find any indication of how long the service has been in business, be wary. If a service has been around for a while (over five years), it's a good indication.
4. **Is there a sample audit you can examine?** You can tell a lot about the skills of auditors by the reports they produce. Ask for one if you can't find one on the Web. If you are unable to get a sample, be wary.
5. **Is the audit methodology posted publicly?** Auditing services that know what they are doing will post their methods for everyone to see.
6. **Are there a variety of services to choose from?** The more reputable services will include a variety of audit options, training for different audiences, website accessibility monitoring, and other services that approach web accessibility from many angles.
7. **Is the service's website accessible?** Reputable services will lead by example. Their websites will be spotless from an accessibility perspective and the HTML of the site should validate.

Third-Party Web Accessibility Auditing

It may be beneficial for both the vendor and the procuring organization to have a third-party accessibility auditing service brought in to provide an unbiased review of the software being acquired. This requirement may be part of a contractual agreement that requires confirmation of compliance with a given standard from an expert working at arm's length from the two parties. It provides a level of protection for both parties, providing an objective account of a software's state of accessibility that both parties can refer to if disagreement should arise.

A Few Reputable Accessibility Auditing Services

Here are a few web accessibility auditing services known to be reputable:

- Deque Systems
- The Paciello Group
- WebSavvy (Inclusive Design Research Centre)
- Level Access

Contract for Accessibility

Assuming you have received proposals from vendors, tested their understanding of web accessibility, and are ready to move into a contractual arrangement to license or purchase the software or web application from one of them, it is important to lay out web accessibility requirements in the issued contract.

The following are two approaches to defining accessibility requirements: the first is a more **general approach**, relying on a specific standard to which vendors can refer, and the second is a more **detailed approach**, which relies on a standard but also supplies specific requirements that must be met.

Section 508 Wording

The National Center on Disability and Access to Education (NCDAE) provides some standard text for contracts that makes accessibility a requirement of the agreement. This text will be relevant for those procuring under the Section 508 regulations:

> **Sample 1: Purchasing contracts of specific products**
> Vendors must ensure that the course management system contained in the proposal fully conforms with Section 508 of the Rehabilitation Act of 1973, as amended in 2017. (For information on Section 508, see www.section508.gov.) This includes both the student and instructor views and also includes all interaction tools (e.g., chats, discussion forums), and add-ons (e.g., grade functions). Vendors must declare if any portion of the version under consideration does not fully conform to Section 508, and the ways in which the proposed product is out of compliance.

Source: The National Center on Disability and Access to Education

While this approach may be sufficient in some cases, where it has been confirmed that the vendor understands the requirements of Section 508, there will be cases when vendors don't know if their product conforms or not. To reduce that likelihood, details of the Section 508 requirements could be specified, something like the requirements outlined in the "WCAG 2.0 Wording" section below.

WCAG 2.0 Wording

Like the wording for RFPs introduced earlier in this unit, it is important for contracts to provide specific details in order to avoid potential confusion for vendors who may not be fully aware of WCAG 2.0 requirements. The following is an adapted version of the Section 508 wording above, with suggested wording that specifies an agreed upon course of action should accessibility issues be discovered after the contract is implemented, along with the procuring organization's specific accessibility requirements. Though WCAG 2.0 is specified, this language would be **appropriate for those drafting AODA-related web accessibility requirements.**

Sample 2: Purchasing contracts of specific products Vendors must ensure that the course management system contained in the proposal fully conforms with the Web Content Accessibility Guidelines (WCAG 2.0), Level AA, as published by the Web Accessibility Initiative (WAI) of the W3C, summarized in the list below (see WCAG 2.0 for more information). This includes both the student and instructor views and also includes all interaction tools (e.g., chats, discussion forums), and add-ons (e.g., grade functions). Vendors must declare if any portion of the version under consideration does not fully conform to WCAG 2.0 Level AA, and describe the ways in which the proposed product is out of compliance.Vendors agree that their product will continue to conform with these requirements, and in the event potential violations are discovered, will arrange to have such issues resolved unless otherwise agreed upon exceptions are stated in writing.

G1.1.1 (Level A)

All meaningful images in the User Interface (UI) include a text alternative, in the form of alt text, that accurately describes the meaning or function associated with the image.

G1.2.2 (Level A)

Where video is provided, either in the product itself, or in the associated documentation, meaningful spoken dialog in the video includes closed captions produced by a person rather than an automated service.

G 1.3.1 (Level A)

Content is structured using proper HTML section headings (e.g., h1, h2) and proper lists (i.e., ol, ul, li) rather than formatting that just creates the appearance of a heading or list.

G 1.3.2 (Level A)

When navigating through elements of the UI and content using only the Tab key, the cursor takes a logical path, from left to right and from top to bottom.

G 1.4.1 (Level A)

When colour is used in a meaningful way, some method other than colour is used to represent that same meaning.

G 1.4.3 (Level AA)

When text is presented over a coloured background, a minimum contrast between the two of 4.5:1 for standard sized text, and 3:1 for larger text, is provided.

G 2.1.1 (Level A)

All elements in the UI or content that function with a mouse click, also function using only a keyboard.

G 2.4.1 (Level A)

Means are provided that allow assistive technology users, or keyboard only users, to skip past repetitive elements such as menus and navigation bars, using either bypass links, or WAI-ARIA landmarks.

G 2.4.4 (Level A)

All link text is meaningful either on its own, or within the context of other adjacent links, accurately describing the destination or function of the link.

G 3.3.1 (Level A)

Error messages are presented in a way that can be consumed by assistive technology without requiring the user to search through the content to find them, either presented consistently in one place on the page or using an ARIA alert role.

G 3.3.2 (Level A)

Forms are formatted in a way that explicitly associates labels with input fields, and sufficient instructions are provided to describe the expected input in each field.

G 2.4.7 (Level AA)

When navigating through the UI using the tab key only, the focus position is easily followed visually through elements on the screen.

G 4.1.1 (Level A)

(**Exception**: Meets this requirement to the extent that markup violations do not introduce barriers that affect access for assistive technologies.)

The markup of the UI complies with HTML5 specifications.

Vendor Declaration of Non-Compliance [Vendor declares here any aspects of the product that are known to be non-compliant with WCAG 2.0 Level AA requirements, to be acknowledged by the procuring organization and either agreed upon as exceptions, or to be resolved within a particular time period following the implementation of the contract.]

Working with Vendors

Now that you have a contractual agreement in place with a particular vendor, you will want to maintain a working relationship with them through which any accessibility issues that may be introduced into the product, either through software updates or through issues discovered after the contract is in place, can be resolved with minimal aggravation.

Fortunately, with the introduction of accessibility laws in many jurisdictions, vendors and suppliers are becoming more aware of accessibility issues and recognize that improving the accessibility of their products is good for business. As such, vendors are often receptive to accessibility improvements to their products. Your organization can potentially provide free user testing through feedback from your own employees or clients.

Talking About Web Accessibility with Vendors

How you approach your discussion of accessibility with vendors will vary depending on the level of awareness the vendor already has. You should already have an idea of the vendor's understanding through the assessments you have already done, reviewing the company's website, and if you are at the proposal stage, through responses to the requirements laid out in the RFP.

You will generally want to start the accessibility discussion right at the beginning of the procurement process. If there is work to be done to improve accessibility, the best approach is to address it from the start, rather than having to go back and retrofit after other details of a potential contract have been worked through.

There are several *approaches* to the accessibility **discussion with vendors**, which range from:

- Putting the onus on your company, the procuring organization, and its responsibility to provide accessible products and service (**We can't buy from you if you are not accessible**)
- Stating the business case, selling the idea that accessibility is good for the vendor through increased sales and improved efficiency (**Your revenues will increase, and/or your costs will decrease**)
- Stating the legal case, reducing the likelihood of legal action for discriminating against people with disabilities (**You are less likely to be sued**)
- Making the social-conscience case or positioning the vendor as a company that should demonstrate corporate responsibility. (**It's the right thing to do**)

The above may all sound familiar to you if you think back to **the business cases** introduced early. There are a number of other discussions you can employ to build a vendor's accessibility awareness:

- **Accessibility is practice, not a touch-up.** Addressing accessibility from the start requires little extra effort once you know what you're doing. Retrofitting can be difficult, expensive, or even impossible.
- **Standards are clear, and adopted all over the world.** Companies are adopting standards such as WCAG as a business advantage. Many buyers have accessibility at the top of their procurement requirements, and will often skip over suppliers that are not addressing it.
- **Show your accessibility.** For those in the U.S., if you do not have a VPAT, it will likely affect your bottom line. Purchasers may bypass your company if they can't find one. In other areas of the world, providing an "accessibility statement" demonstrates to purchaser's that accessibility is a priority, and a well-thought-out statement is more

likely to cause purchasers to look at your company more closely.

- **We can help you become accessible.** If your organization knows what it needs in terms of accessibility, share that knowledge with potential partner vendors and educate them as part of the process of improving the accessibility of their products so they match the needs of your organization.

Activity: Critique Accessibility Claims

Though specific to the U.S., the Voluntary Product Accessibility Template (VPAT) is a checklist that companies who supply the U.S. government can fill out to document the accessibility of their products. Because a VPAT is completed by the vendor, or a representative of the vendor, they have a tendency to present products in a better light than what may actually be the case. As a result, any time you are presented with a VPAT, or similar accessibility claim, it is important that a person knowledgeable in digital accessibility critically review the document.

> **Toolkit:** Download the VPAT 2.1 form [DOC] and add it to your Toolkit.

Review the Canvas and Blackboard VPATs provided below and write up a critique of each. Note that these are the older VPAT forms, which are based on the requirements of the old Section 508.

1. Canvas LMS VPAT
2. Blackboard Learn VPAT [PDF]

Questions you may want to answer include, but are not limited to:

- Is there missing information or additional information that could have been provided?
- Is there overly complex language used that might confuse a reader with limited accessibility knowledge?
- Are there statements that would cause you to question the validity of the remarks?
- Are there any statements acknowledging known issues?
- Are there explanations that do not appear relevant to the criteria?
- On a scale of 1 to 10, how well do you think the remarks address the given criteria?

Comparing the two VPATs, which would you be more likely to believe is accurate, and why do you think this?

Procurement and Accessibility Policy: Takeaways

In this unit, you learned that:

- To be successful, an effective web accessibility policy should be rooted within the business culture following the WebAIM eight-step process.
- A web accessibility policy should include procurement practices for both IT and non-IT related goods and services.
- Vendors should be able to verify and validate the accessibility compliance of their products and services.

6. HIRING ACCESSIBILITY STAFF

Hiring Accessibility Staff

This final unut will expand on the discussion of policy introduced in Unit 5. One of the key elements in implementing web accessibility policy is hiring staff that possess accessibility knowledge and ensuring they know how accessibility fits into their roles.

Hiring staff explicitly to implement and manage accessibility efforts is perhaps the most important indicator that an organization is committed to developing and maintaining products and services that are inclusive. There are two particular roles that we will examine here: the **Web Developer** and the **Web/IT Accessibility Specialist**. These two roles are generally responsible for the bulk of compliance efforts undertaken in an organization.

Despite our focus on these two roles in particular, it is important to remember that accessibility can and should be a part of a company's regular business practices, with staff at all levels contributing to the maintenance of an organization's accessibility status.

Video: Making the world accessible | Dave Power | TEDxBeaconStreet

A YouTube element has been excluded from this version of the text. You can view it online here: https://pressbooks.library.ryerson.ca/dabp/?p=770

Objectives and Activities

Objectives

By the end of this unit, you should be able to:

- Identify accessibility knowledge and skills needed across organizational roles.
- Develop an organizational rationale for hiring people with disabilities.
- State accessibility skills required by web developers.
- Identify job descriptions for hiring accessibility professionals.

Activities

- Find an accessibility professional job description.
- Complete the Sharp Clothing Company digital accessibility policy.

Hiring Knowledgable Staff

It is clear to you that web developers need to have a good understanding of accessibility, as they will be responsible for much of the company's digital accessibility. But, you also want to understand what knowledge and skills other staff should have, so you can ask the appropriate accessibility questions during job interviews with potential candidates.

Roles and Accessibility Responsibilities

For most positions an organization may be hiring for, digital accessibility knowledge or skills need not be a requirement, though having that knowledge or skills should add points to a candidate's overall score. For most positions, a little training will provide the needed details of accessibility requirements for particular roles.

Of the various roles that could be found in an organization, it is the web developers who will need to be most familiar with accessibility requirements and the strategies to meet those requirements. Knowledge and skills for web developers will be covered separately later in this unit.

The following lists in general terms the skills and knowledge each role in an organization should possess or be trained in, starting with knowledge everyone should possess and followed by additional specific skills for particular roles:

Everyone

- Disability sensitivity
- Organization requirements (high level, legislated obligations)

Senior managers

- Organization requirements (details of legislated obligations)
- Experience with change-management projects

Store managers

- Customer-service accessibility

Sales staff

- Customer-service accessibility

Office staff

- Document accessibility
- Basic web accessibility

Human resource staff

- Role-based accessibility knowledge and skills
- Accessible employment practices and local accessibility regulations
- Document accessibility
- Knowledge of training, change management
- Knowledge of accommodations for people with disabilities
- Knowledge of the organization's accessibility efforts

Communication and marketing

- Document accessibility
- Multimedia accessibility
- Basic web accessibility

Purchasers

- Organization requirements (procurement)
- Basic web accessibility

Telephone support staff

- Customer service accessibility

UI designer

- Universal design principles
- Basic web accessibility

Web content authors

- Basic web accessibility

Media support staff

- Basic web accessibility
- Multimedia accessibility

Distribution centre staff

- Minimal

Cleaning and maintenance

- Minimal

Readings & Resources: Accessibility Job Descriptions

Hiring People with Disabilities

After reviewing the staff list when looking into training for various roles, you discover the company employs only one person who has identified as having a disability. Given approximately 15% of the population has a disability, you think the company is missing an opportunity to benefit from diversifying its workforce by leveraging this relatively untapped talent pool. You also realize that hiring additional staff with a visible disability will help spread awareness of the need for digital accessibility throughout the company. You make the following recommendation to the accessibility committee: The company should make an effort to hire an accessibility quality-assurance person to test products for accessibility, provide input on the company's accessibility practices, and help expose staff to people with disabilities to raise awareness of the need for digital accessibility. You suggest hiring a qualified person, who is blind and uses a screen reader to access the web and other digital information, into a new office support role.

Video: David Onley, Lieutenant Governor of Ontario: Business Case for Hiring People with Disabilities

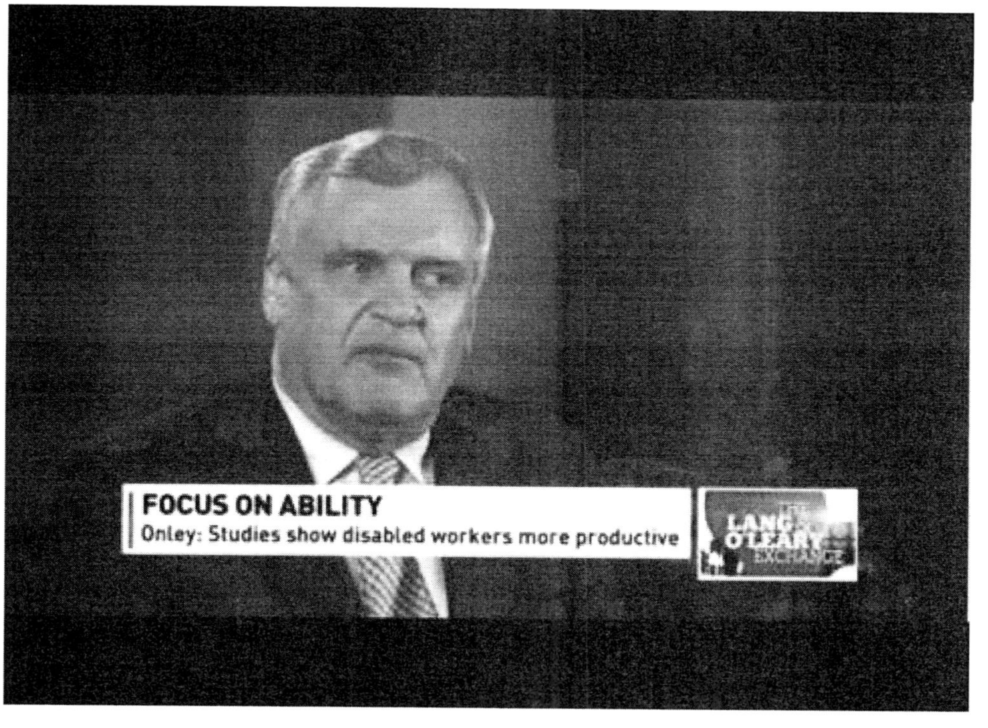

A YouTube element has been excluded from this version of the text. You can view it online here: https://pressbooks.library.ryerson.ca/dabp/?p=777

Addressing Myths About Hiring People with Disabilities

Although there are many well-educated, skilled people with disabilities in Canada and in other countries around the world, they continue to be unemployed, or underemployed at a rate more than twice that of the general adult population. In fact according to Human Resources and Skills Development Canada, more than 50% of people with disabilities have high school diplomas, and over one third of these have completed a post-secondary program.

In Ontario, the unemployment rate for people with disabilities is about 8% higher than the general population, as reported by the Ontario Chamber of Commerce (OCC). According to the OCC, this is in part due to systemic and cultural discrimination based on misperceptions of people with disabilities. People with disabilities are often perceived as less productive, more likely to take time off, too costly to accommodate, and more likely to be a burden on employees who do not have disabilities. In fact the opposite is true for all these points. Because people with disabilities have more difficulty finding work, they are likely to value employment more than typical fully abled workers.

The Ontario Chamber of Commerce has put together a list of eight myths about hiring people with disabilities, and the OCC challenges those myths with facts. Take a few moments to read through "8 Myths About Hiring People with Disabilities."

Readings & References:

- 8 Myths About Hiring People with Disabilities
- Disability Facts and the Labour Force (HRSDC)

Accessible Hiring Practices

In Ontario, the employment standards of the AODA describes requirements for accessible employment practices, from recruitment procedures, to employee accommodations, to performance management, and more. As of January 1, 2017, all organizations in Ontario, including small ones, must meet the AODA employment standards's requirements. These requirements are summarized below:

1. Notify employees and the public about the availability of job accommodations for applicants with disabilities.
2. Ensure that the methods being used to advertise employment vacancies are inclusive, with alternative formats available where appropriate.
3. Notify prospective applicants that interview accommodations are available upon request.
4. If an applicant requests accommodation, consult with the applicant on suitable ways to provide those accommodations.
5. Upon making a job offer, and upon start of employment, notify candidates of policies for accommodating employees with disabilities.
6. Upon request, provide information in accessible formats to employees needed to perform their job, as well as information generally available to employees.
7. Provide personalized emergency-response information that takes into account employees's disabilities, and to a designated assistant if one is required. Review emergency-response information if an employee moves or changes jobs.

8. Have a process in place to document individual accommodation plans (other than small organizations).
9. Upon return to work due to disability, develop an accommodation plan for employees returning after an absence.
10. During performance reviews, take into account employee disabilities, accessibility needs, and individual accommodation plans.
11. When career development is provided, take into account employee disabilities, accessibility needs, and individual accommodation plans.
12. When redeployment is provided, take into account employee disabilities, accessibility needs, and individual accommodation plans.

Readings & References: AODA Employment Standards

Employee Accommodation

For employees with disabilities, employed in a role that involves consuming or producing digital information, accommodations typically include supplying assistive technologies that provide access to a computer. If employees with disabilities do not already have a preferred means of accommodation, they will often receive a workplace accommodation assessment, typically conducted by an occupational therapist (OC). The OC will recommend adjustments to workspaces to accommodate a disability, as well as assistive software or hardware to make possible or aid with tasks associated with particular roles that involve using a computer.

The following is a list of potential accommodations that may be required by people with disabilities. In most cases accommodation will cost less than $1000, sometimes much less.

PEOPLE WHO ARE BLIND

People who are blind will typically require a screen reader to access a computer, which reads aloud the information on a computer screen. If they are deafblind, or for blind users who read Braille, they may also require a refreshable Braille display working along with a screen reader to turn text on a computer screen into raised dots on a finger pad that refreshes while navigating through the text.

PEOPLE WITH LOW VISION

People with low vision may or may not require a screen reader. Some will require magnification software, while others will rely on magnification built into the operating system or web browsers they may be using.

PEOPLE WHO ARE DEAF OR HARD OF HEARING

For those with loss of hearing, they may not require assistive technology beyond hearing aids. They may, however, require audio content in alternative formats, typically written, and they may require accommodations for meetings, either a scribe to take notes or use instant messaging, or perhaps voice recognition software to transcribe spoken words to a computer screen. Real-time captioning services may be an option, connecting by phone or internet to a service that types what is heard to be displayed on a computer screen.

Some people who are Deaf will be able to read lips. For this to be effective, others need to be trained to be aware when they speak, that their lips are in view for the person who is lip reading.

TTY (text telephone or teletypewriter) may also be required if a person who is Deaf will be communicating by telephone. Video-relay services, similar in nature to real-time captions, have a remote interpreter listen and interpret to sign language, displayed on a computer screen.

In some cases, particularly where ASL is the person's first language, a sign-language interpreter may be required. This can be an expensive option, however. Augmentative communication devices might be used as an alternative to sign-language interpreting, used to translate English into ASL.

PEOPLE WITH COGNITIVE DISABILITIES

Cognitive disabilities can be quite varied. Assistive technologies are less likely to be required. Rather job accommodations may be needed, aligning work duties with the capacity to comprehend and complete those duties effectively. People with cognitive disabilities may be well suited to take on entry level duties that are often not challenging enough for others.

Other's with cognitive disabilities such as autism, Asperger's Syndrome, and other pervasive developmental delays (PDDs), can be quite intelligent in some respects, while having difficulties with social interaction. They may be able to take on highly complex, specialized tasks, but may need privacy or routine to function effectively.

PEOPLE WITH LEARNING DISABILITIES

People with learning disabilities are typically as intelligent as others, some more than average. They typically have difficulties in a specific area, such as reading, or mathematics, or interpreting visual input. In some cases, no accommodations are needed. For others, they may required text-to-speech technology to read text aloud.

PEOPLE WITH FINE-MOTOR DISABILITIES

For those who have limited use of their hands, perhaps due to a spinal-cord injury, or perhaps an inability to hold their hand steady enough to handle a keyboard or mouse, a variety of assistive technologies may be employed.

Speech recognition may be required by some, allowing them to speak commands to a computer, or dictate text to a document. For those who cannot handle a mouse or keyboard, technologies such as eye tracking, or a head mouse, might be required to allow them to control a mouse pointer, and press a large button switch that take the place of a mouse click.

Some may require a keyboard with large keys, that are easier to target with a shaky hand. Others may be accommodated with low-tech solutions such as a keyboard cover with holes over each key that prevent adjacent keys from being pressed.

PEOPLE USING A WHEELCHAIR

People using a wheelchair to accommodate loss of movement in their legs typically do not need any assistive technology when interacting with a computer. For those who have loss of movement in the arms and legs, technologies like those described for fine-motor disabilities may be required.

Readings & References:

- Access to Success: A Guide for Employers (NEADS)
- Employers' Toolkit: Making Ontario Workplaces Accessible to People with Disabilities [PDF] (Conference

Board of Canada)

Video: How Creating a Culture of Accessibility Positively Impacts Business

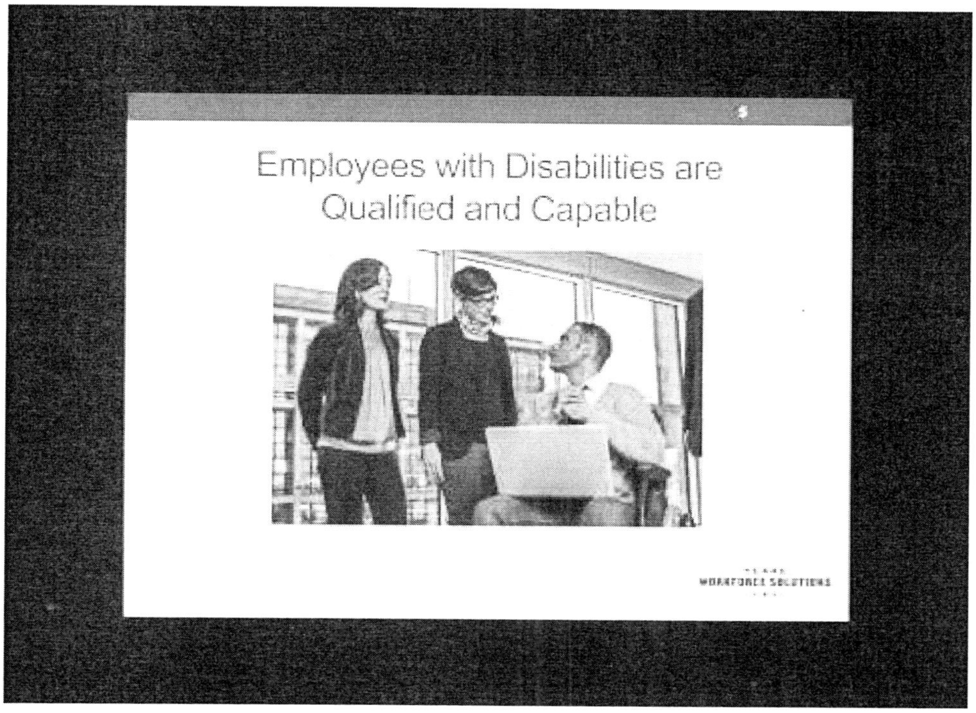

A YouTube element has been excluded from this version of the text. You can view it online here: https://pressbooks.library.ryerson.ca/dabp/?p=777

Accessible Web Developers

In terms of web accessibility, it is the web developer who must be knowledgeable in implementing accessibility in web content. As much as others may understand how and where barriers can affect access, it is the developer who makes accessibility happen. A web developer usually has a university-level computer science degree and/or special training in developing for the Web.

Currently, there are few formal technical programs that provide anything more than cursory coverage of web accessibility. As such, web developers who are qualified to implement accessibility are often self-taught. Finding a web developer with expert accessibility skills can be a challenge, and it may mean settling for a person who simply knows the basics about web accessibility. If you plan to hire a web/IT accessibility specialist, hiring web developers with knowledge of accessibility is less of an issue, since the specialist can oversee the work of the developers and guide or train them (see the next page for further details).

Web Developers' Accessibility Skills

In addition to the skills that might be part of a standard job description for a web developer, an Accessible Web Developer should also have these characteristics:

- Skilled use of HTML, CSS, and JavaScript
- Good understanding of WCAG 2.0, or local accessibility guidelines
- Knowledge of WAI-ARIA (preferably skilled use of)
- Ability to effectively use JAWS or another screen reader
- Familiarity with mobile screen readers
- Familiarity with automated web-accessibility checking tools
- Familiarity with browser-based accessibility-testing tools (plugins, etc.)
- Knowledge of accessibility issues in technologies such as Flash and Java
- Knowledge of cross-browser accessibility considerations

If you can find a web developer with expert understanding and all the skills needed to implement accessibility, hire that person. But, chances are you will find people with some, but not all of these characteristics. Hire the ones with the broadest backgrounds who are resourceful enough to find answers to accessibility problems based on familiarity with web accessibility as a whole.

Video: IT Accessibility: What Web Developers Have to Say

A YouTube element has been excluded from this version of the text. You can view it online here: https://pressbooks.library.ryerson.ca/dabp/?p=780

Web/IT Accessibility Specialist

The web/IT accessibility specialist has a key role in the development of organizational accessibility culture. This person is often a manager with a technical background or a web developer, knowledgeable of accessibility and disability issues, whose role it is to oversee an organization's web and IT accessibility efforts.

Much like web developers with accessibility expertise, accessibility specialists can also be difficult to find and they are often self-taught. They come from varied backgrounds and through experience working with people with disabilities and assistive technologies, they develop a unique awareness of accessibility and what that means from technical, social, economic, political, and educational perspectives.

Accessibility Specialist Knowledge and Skills

The range of skills and knowledge will vary from specialist to specialist, though there are some core characteristics to look for, and a range of additional skills that will be outlined here. Duties may also vary, depending on the organization's requirements. The following is a generic list of duties and potential characteristics for a web/IT accessibility specialist. A variation of these characteristics may apply in different circumstances, whether you are working in the business or corporate world, in education, in government, or in the accessibility services field.

DUTIES

- Manage and/or implement web accessibility efforts throughout the organization
- Accessibility quality control of documents, websites, and IT systems
- Train staff from varied backgrounds (e.g., customer service, sales, developers, and managers)
- Develop documentation and training materials for diverse groups within the organization
- Report accessibility/research efforts to senior management/stakeholders
- Provide assistive technology guidance for clients or staff with disabilities
- Present accessibility/research efforts at relevant conferences or meetings (this item is more specific to the educational sector)
- Write and publish accessibility/research efforts (this item is more specific to the educational sector)
- Participate in international standards working groups that promote accessibility

MINIMUM CORE KNOWLEDGE

- Strong background in web development
- Expert knowledge of WCAG 2.0
- Project management skills
- Functional knowledge of WAI-ARIA (expertise would be an asset)
- Knowledge of accessibility features across a full range of operating systems
- Experience teaching or training adult learners
- Familiarity with mobile and desktop screen readers
- Familiarity with automated accessibility checkers
- Graduate degree or better, in a related field or equivalent practical experience

- Ability to interact effectively with junior and senior staff, government and the public
- Strong oral communication skills
- Technical writing skills

ADDITIONAL SKILLS

- Knowledge of a range of assistive technologies and devices
- Knowledge of UI design, implementation and testing
- Knowledge of disabilities, and disability sensitivity
- Functional knowledge of ATAG 2.0 and UAAG 2.0 specifications
- Familiarity with international accessibility and disability regulations
- Well networked with the global accessibility community
- Qualitative research background (user studies)

Readings & References: For examples of web/IT Accessibility Specialist job descriptions, review the following resources:

- Sample IT Accessibility Specialist Job Description [PDF]
- Sample Web Accessibility Position Description [PDF]
- Additional IT Accessibility Job Descriptions

Self-Test 8

1. When hiring a new graduate web developer, they should list at least one course they took on web accessibility.
    1. True
    2. False
2. Workplace accommodations for a person who is blind would typically include which of the following technologies? Choose all that apply.
    1. Screen reader
    2. Voice recognition
    3. Trackball
    4. Text-to-speech
    5. Screen magnification

Answer Key to Self-Test 8

An interactive or media element has been excluded from this version of the text. You can view it online here: https://pressbooks.library.ryerson.ca/dabp/?p=786

Accessibility Interview Questions

When hiring staff, you can question them about their general accessibility knowledge during the interview process. Though typically not a requirement for most jobs, accessibility knowledge and skills should be an asset when considering candidates. For most roles, except perhaps web developer or procurement roles, role-related accessibility knowledge and skills can be learned with a little training. Web developers and purchasers will require a much broader understanding than most other roles.

Below are examples of the types of questions that might be asked, grouped by the knowledge area or skill type, with suggested answers. This is not an exhaustive list.

> **Toolkit:** Accessibility Interview Questions [PDF]

Disability Sensitivity

(Also see Customer Service section below)

When a blind person using a white cane, enters your store, how should you approach that person, and/or offer assistance?
If the person appears to be be having difficulty, ask first "Can I help you?" If the person answers yes, ask "How can I help you best?" and follow their lead. Never assume a blind person, or any other person with a disability, needs help. Some people will not want to be helped, preferring independence.

When a blind person enters your store with a service dog, how should you address the dog entering your store or restaurant?
The dog is working, and should be ignored. Do not pet the dog, or address the dog directly unless the person suggests you may. The dog must be allowed in the store or restaurant, though may be denied access to food-preparation areas.

You catch yourself saying "we'll see each other later" to a blind person, or you catch yourself saying "we have to run" to a person in a wheelchair. How should you respond to these sayings?
You do not need to respond. Phrases like these are a natural part of daily life, and people with disabilities will not be offended by them. They may, however, be offended by apologizing for the phrase.

Organizational Requirements (Basic)

What accessibility regulations affect businesses in Ontario (or some other location)?
In Ontario, candidates should mention AODA. Bonus if IASR is mentioned or the standards that make up this regulation.

In the U.S., mention section 508 of the Rehabilitation Act and the Americans with Disabilities Act (ADA).

Refer to International Digital Accessibility Regulations in Unit 2, for regulations in other parts of the world.

When are organizations in Ontario (or elsewhere) with 50+ employees required make their websites accessible?

In Ontario, they should mention January 1, 2014, bonus if they mention Level A, added bonus if they mention Level AA by 2021.

Organizational Requirements (Detailed)

Which standard of the IASR (AODA) governs digital accessibility requirements?
The Information and Communication Standard.

What standard are the web accessibility requirements of The Information and Communication Standard, and other regulations around the world, typically governed by?
The W3C Web Content Accessibility Guidelines (WCAG 2.0)

For organizations over 50 employees, what are the reporting requirements under AODA?
Section 4 of the regulation requires each obligated organization to establish and implement a multi-year plan describing how it will achieve its accessibility requirements under the regulation, and post that plan to their website (if they have one). Plans must be reviewed and updated every five years.

Customer Service

When a person who is deaf is communicating with you through a sign interpreter, how should you reply?
Reply directly to the person, not to the interpreter. Reply like you would reply to any person, looking directly at the person with your mouth clearly in view. Enunciate words clearly and, if requested, slow speech slightly to allow those who can lip read to more easily visually interpret.

If approached by a person with a prosthesis on their right arm, how should you shake hands with that person?
Shaking the left hand would be appropriate, or wait for the person to extend a hand. If a person is unable to shake hands, touch them lightly on the shoulder or arm to greet them.

An adult person with a cognitive impairment (e.g., Down syndrome) asks you for help. How should you respond?
Respond to that person as you would any other adult customer. You may want to slow your speech slightly and speak clearly. Do not speak to the person as if they were a child. Do not speak through a family member who might be with the person.

A person in a wheelchair has approached you asking about a particular product that requires an extended description. What might you do to provide a respectful answer?
Talk to the person like any other adult. If there is an opportunity to sit, pull up a chair and address the person eye to eye.

A person with a speech impairment is asking you in a stuttered voice, about the prices for a number of items, but is having difficulty getting the words out. How should you respond?
Be patient, and allow the person to finish speaking their question. Do not attempt to finish their sentences for them. Do not pretend to understand if you don't. It is okay to say "I'm not sure I understand." If they try again and you are still unable to understand, ask if the person would like to write the question, if the person is able.

Basic Web Accessibility

How would you make an image in a web page accessible to someone who is blind?
Add alt text to the image HTML to describe the meaningful elements of the image and, if necessary, provide a more detailed description in a caption or in the surrounding text.

When writing an article for the Web, how would you go about structuring the document to make it usable by someone using a screen reader?
Use proper HTML headings to organize sections and subsections, instead of using large bold text. Use proper list HTML to organize items arranged in a list, rather than using asterisks or separating items with a new line.

Document Accessibility

When preparing a Microsoft Word document, what can be done to make the document accessible to people who are blind?
Provide text descriptions for images. Arrange content using proper headings. Use table headers when presenting data in tables.

How would you make a PDF document accessible to a blind person, reading it with a screen reader?
If exported from Microsoft Word, make the Word document accessible first. Open the exported PDF in a current version of Adobe Acrobat Pro, and use its accessibility features to adjust the document. Use the reading order feature in Acrobat Pro to adjust the order in which the parts of each page are read, if necessary.

Role-Based Knowledge

What accessibility knowledge is needed by staff who are producing documents for public distribution?
Be able to use the accessibility test tools in Word or in Acrobat Pro, for example, to test and make adjustments to documents. Must be aware of accessibility features in document authoring tools, such as how to add alt text for images or create table headers.

When hiring counter/sales staff, what knowledge of accessibility/disability is needed?
They must be sensitive to people with disabilities. Speak to people with disabilities like you would speak to anyone else. Ask before attempting to help. Sit, if possible, when having a conversation with a person in a wheelchair. Do not interact with service animals. Speak directly to the person with a disability, not through their support person. Must be familiar with local customer service accessibility laws.

What accessibility knowledge or skills is needed by a person being hired for a web development position?
Web developers must be familiar with WCAG (specifically, principles, levels, success criteria, and techniques). Should be able to name a screen reader or two for accessibility testing (e.g., JAWS, NVDA, Window Eyes, ChromeVox, and others). Must be familiar with accessibility testing tools (and name a few, and what they are used for). Should be familiar with WAI-ARIA, used when developing interactive elements in websites or web applications. Understanding issues associated with mouse and keyboard access. Must be familiar with the types of barriers people with different types of disabilities encounter.

When hiring a manager, what accessibility knowledge do they need?

They must be familiar with the local accessibility laws and be able to describe the legislation and its requirements. They should understand the types of accessibility knowledge that should be possessed by the people reporting to them. They should be familiar with accessibility tools and resources their staff can access.

When hiring a marketing and communications person, what do they need to know about accessibility?
They should have a basic understanding of web and document accessibility, such as providing alternatives for visuals, structuring documents, using tools to test for accessibility. Must understand issues associated with using colour in an accessible way (e.g., contrast, alternatives for colour with meaning).

When hiring a human-resource person, what do they need to know about accessibility?
Human-resource people should be aware of role-based accessibility knowledge required for an organization's various roles.

Accessible Employment Practices

What can be done to ensure that people with disabilities have an equal opportunity to apply for jobs as their able peers?
Employers should inform applicants that accommodations are available on request in relation to materials and processes used.

If accommodations are requested, the employer must consult with the applicant on suitable accommodations that account for the applicant's disability.

If hired, the hiring notification sent to the applicant will take into consideration the applicant's disability and include the organization's policy for accommodating employees with disabilities.

Multimedia

What potential accommodations can be included with video to ensure it is accessible to people with disabilities?
To accommodate people who are deaf, captions can be included.

To accommodate people who are blind, audio description, or extended audio description can be added to video that describe actions or the context, that might otherwise not be understood by listening to the audio track of a video.

What potential accommodations can be included with audio to ensure it is accessible to people with disabilities?
To accommodate people who are deaf, a transcript can be included with audio.

Universal Design

In what ways does universal design address web accessibility for people with disabilities, while at the same time improving usability for everyone?
This can potentially be a long list. These are some examples:

- Create link text that is meaningful, avoiding links like "click here." Able and disabled people can scan links of a page

more easily without having to follow links to see where they lead.
- Prevent errors from occurring using effective prompting, feedback messaging, and data validation. Ensures everyone is prevented from submitting incorrect data.
- When presenting visual content, also include text describing the meaningful element of the visual. Provide a text description for those who cannot see and describe the visual for those who might not understand the meaningful elements of the visual.
- Use relative measures to size elements in web content so it easily adapts to magnification, and to a variety of device screen sizes.
- Include redundant modalities, such as including a visual cue, like a flash, when an audio cue, like a beep, is presented, for those who cannot hear, or those who have audio turned down.

> **Toolkit:** Other examples of universal design for a accessibility

Procurement

When purchasing software to be used on a website, when is it appropriate to use software that may not be accessibility compliant?
When no accessible alternative exists.

When the cost is excessive and would create undue hardship for the organization.

Otherwise, when comparable products are available to choose from, the more accessible option should be procured.

What questions should be asked in a Request for Proposals (RFPs), when purchasing software to be used on the Web?
This can potentially be a long list. These are some examples:

- Can the software be used effectively without the need to use a mouse?
- Can the software be magnified to at least 200% (and 400%) using browser settings, without information being lost off the side of the screen?
- Does contrast between text and background throughout the user interface meet WCAG 2 requirements?
- What testing was done to ensure the user interface of your application will be usable by people using assistive technology?
- What processes do you have in place to address accessibility issues, should they be discovered after we have licensed your software?

In addition to asking for accessibility in RFPs, what other things must be considered when purchasing software?
This can potentially be a long list. These are some examples:

- Evaluate vendor responses critically. Some may provide answers without experience or knowledge of specific requirements.
- Complete your own testing of the software to confirm vendor claims. Or, ask for an unbiased third party accessibility review.
- Ensure that contractual arrangements address ongoing maintenance of accessibility, for instance, during upgrades or software updates, or when previous undetected accessibility issues are discovered.

Activity: Find an IT Accessibility Professional Job Description

Hiring an accessibility professional and putting together a job description for their position is likely to be an activity an organization will need to undertake in its efforts to develop a culture of accessibility. When you are developing your own accessibility job description, it can be helpful to see what other organizations are looking for in an accessibility professional.

Spend a few moments with your favourite search engine and try to locate examples of job postings for accessibility professionals. Select one or two positions and write up a short summary of them. Include information like the location, company name, salary, years of experience needed, etc.

Here are a few search terms you can use to get started. Use your imagination to come up with other potential search terms that would turn up similar positions. Try adding a city name to your search terms to find positions close to you.

SEARCH TERMS

- IT Accessibility Specialist
- Web Accessibility Specialist
- Web Accessibility Engineer
- Accessibility Expert
- Accessibility Analyst
- Accessibility Program Manager

Note: If you have difficulty locating job postings, but find in your search that you discover profiles of people currently working in the field, take note of those.
Hint: Search LinkedIn

Hiring Accessibility Staff: Takeaways

In this unit, you learned that:

- Companies are missing out on a significant talent pool of highly educated and skilled workers when they exclude people with disabilities in their hiring practices.
- Few formal technical training programs focus on developing accessible web content, creating self-taught specialists, each having some common knowledge as well as informal personal skill sets related to accessible content.

Final Project

1. Activity: Create the Sharp Clothing Company's Digital Accessibility Policy
2. Challenge Test 9

Activity: Create the Sharp Clothing Company's Digital Accessibility Policy

This final activity will bring together all that you have learned throughout the materials here. Think of it as a culminating activity. A digital accessibility policy should be written as a guide that management and staff can use to understand what they need to be doing to meet the organization's accessibility requirements.

The following is a list of potential sections for a policy document. You can start with these, add or remove sections or subsections, provide text for each section explaining the what, how, and/or who the section of the policy applies to, and organize it in a coherent way.

- Background
- Company commitment
- Accessibility committee
  - Scope and responsibilities
  - Authority and enforcement
  - Support
- Guidelines and standards
  - Website development
  - Web content
  - Documents and communications
  - Multimedia
  - Third-party content
- Hiring equity and employment accommodation
- Training and awareness
- Digital accessibility resources
- Procurement
- Accessibility auditing and quality assurance
- Monitoring and periodic reviews
- Reporting
- Policy review

Note: Here is one possible version of the policy: Answer Key.

Challenge Test 9

1. Described in Accessibility Awareness Requirements in Other Organizational Roles, it is important for Management to have the following accessibility related knowledge. Choose all that apply.
    1. Knowledge of local and relevant international accessibility related regulations
    2. Knowledge of accessibility policy
    3. Knowledge of disabilities, and associated barriers
    4. Document accessibility (e.g., invoices, receipts, product specifications)
    5. User Interface accessibility design
2. Which of the following would be a typical accommodation for a person with fine-motor impairment. Choose all that apply.
    1. Speech recognition software
    2. Eye tracking hardware
    3. Button switch hardware
    4. Large-key keyboard
    5. Screen reader software
    6. Screen magnification software
    7. Head mouse hardware

Answer Key to Challenge Test 9

An interactive or media element has been excluded from this version of the text. You can view it online here: https://pressbooks.library.ryerson.ca/dabp/?p=86

Content Recap

Unit 1 Summary

This unit is aimed at getting you familiar with the materials and how to make the most of this learning experience.

Unit 2 Summary

In this unit, you learned the following points about understanding accessibility:

- When a business addresses digital accessibility, it actually saves money and doing so is not a non-recoverable cost to the business.
- There is a strong potential for a significant increase in customers for businesses that address digital accessibility.
- Digital accessibility should not be an afterthought but rather it needs to be part of the business strategy and the daily operations of the business.
- Addressing accessibility is a quality attribute of business and improves its profile.

Unit 3 Summary

In this unit, you learned these aspects about establishing a digital accessibility committee:

- Disability sensitivity training, a good understanding of accessibility and standards such as WCAG, and accessibility barriers are all key knowledge areas required in different company roles.
- Accessibility committee members should be chosen strategically and should represent a good cross-section of the business.

Unit 4 Summary

In this unit, you learned the following about creating a digital accessibility culture:

- Accessibility auditing is an important step. Choosing a reputable service involves careful consideration focusing on key reputability factors.
- Two approaches to accessible websites are retrofitting and starting over. The correct approach for your situation will need to consider several factors including outsourcing the work to external vendors.
- Building a company-wide strategy about accessibility includes building awareness, hiring people with disabilities, focused presentations, and training.
- *Web development accessibility* guidelines focus on user interaction with a website whereas *web content accessibility* guidelines focus more on standards compliance. Both are important.
- Several approaches should be used to monitor adherence to accessibility guidelines including unbiased quality assurance reviews and the use of automated tools.

- Implementing accessibility will include managing change. Kotter's Eight-Step Model for Leading Change and Lewin's Three-Step Model are two common models that can help when planning and facilitating the implementation.
- Resistance by staff may be the most challenging element in implementing change and overcoming the five main reasons people resist change needs to be part of your change management strategy.

Unit 5 Summary

In this unit, you learned the following about procurement and accessibility policy:

- To be successful, an effective web accessibility policy should be rooted within the business culture following the WebAIM eight-step process.
- A web accessibility policy should include procurement practices for both IT and non-IT related goods and services.
- Vendors should be able to verify and validate the accessibility compliance of their products and services.

Unit 6 Summary

In this unit, you learned the following points about hiring accessibility staff:

- Companies are missing out on a significant talent pool of highly educated and skilled workers when they exclude people with disabilities in their hiring practices.
- Few formal technical training programs focus on developing accessible web content thus creating self-taught specialists who teach themselves independently. These specialists will have some common knowledge as well as informal personal skill sets related to accessible content.

Web Accessibility Toolkit for Business

Elements in Your Toolkit

Toolkit:

- AODA Definitions and Compliance Timelines [PDF]
- 10 Key Guidelines [PDF]
- Integrate Accessibility Standards Regulation
- Canadian Government Standard on Web Accessibility
- AChecker Web Accessibility Checker
- WAVE Accessibility Checker
- Professional Web Accessibility Auditing Made Easy course
- Accessible Information and Communication: A Guide for Small Businesses
- The WAI-ARIA Workshop
- Web Accessibility Workshop
- Accessibility Hands-On Workshop
- Accessibility Statement Generator
- Sample Vendor Accessibility Compliance Checklist [PDF]
- VPAT Template
- Accessibility Interview Questions [PDF]

Answer Key: Self-Tests

Self-Test 1

1. In Ontario, which section of the AODA Information and Communication Standards addresses website and web content accessibility?
   1. [incorrect] Section 6
   2. [incorrect] Section 12
   3. [incorrect] Section 13
   4. [correct] Section 14
   5. [incorrect] Section 18
2. In the U.S., when are obligated organizations required to comply with the recent changes to Section 508 of the *Rehabilitation Act*?
   1. [incorrect] January 1, 2019
   2. [incorrect] January 1, 2018
   3. [correct] January 18, 2018
   4. [incorrect] March 17, 2017
   5. [incorrect] January 1, 2017

Back to Self-Test 1

Self-Test 2

1. Of the following roles, which need a good understanding of WCAG 2.0, as opposed to a basic understanding? Choose all that apply.
   1. [incorrect] Graphic artists
   2. [correct] Web developers
   3. [incorrect] Web content editors
   4. [incorrect] Video support staff
   5. [correct] Procurement and purchasing staff
   6. [incorrect] Retail store staff
2. Which of the following should be goals and responsibilities of an accessibility committee? Choose all that apply.
   1. [incorrect] Planning the annual company golf tournament.
   2. [correct] Raising accessibility awareness
   3. [correct] Representing the organization in public affairs related to accessibility
   4. [correct] Encouraging feedback to share problems and solutions
   5. [correct] Developing internal accessibility standards
   6. [correct] Implementing accessibility in quality assurance procedures
   7. [correct] Consulting on legal matters related to accessibility
   8. [correct] Providing web and digital accessibility support

Back to Self-Test 2

Self-Test 3

1. Which of the following factors might you take into consideration when selecting a service to audit the accessibility of your organization's website? Choose all that apply.
    1. [correct] How long the firm has been in business.
    2. [correct] Does the firm's auditing processes align with W3C accessibility auditing best practices?
    3. [correct] Does the firm provide automated self-assessment tools for accessibility checking?
    4. [correct] Does the firm offer training for your staff?
    5. [incorrect] Do auditing staff have a university accessibility degree?
2. When self-assessing web accessibility, which of the following are strategies that might be used? Choose all that apply.
    1. [correct] Conduct a Tab key test.
    2. [correct] Use automated accessibility checkers.
    3. [correct] Assign people with disabilities to carry out testing.
    4. [correct] Use a screen reader to navigate through a website.
    5. [correct] Conduct colour contrast testing using an online tool.

Back to Self-Test 3

Self-Test 4

1. When recommending accessibility requirements for web developers, it is best to send them directly to WCAG, on the W3C website.
    1. [incorrect] True
    2. [correct] False
2. When recommending guidelines for staff that produce PDF documents, WCAG should be suggested.
    1. [incorrect] True
    2. [correct] False

Back to Self-Test 4

Self-Test 5

1. Lewin's change model includes eight key steps for managing change.
    1. [incorrect] True
    2. [correct] False
2. Of the following, which one is not a stage of the Kotter Model?
    1. [incorrect] Communicate the Vision

2. [incorrect] Create Urgency
3. [correct] Misunderstanding
4. [incorrect] Create Short-Term Wins

Back to Self-Test 5

Self-Test 6

1. How many steps does the WebAIM accessibility policy implementation model have?
    1. [incorrect] 5
    2. [incorrect] 6
    3. [incorrect] 7
    4. [correct] 8
    5. [incorrect] 9
    6. [incorrect] 10
2. When creating an accessibility statement, which of the following were mentioned as elements that might be included in the statement? Choose all that apply.
    1. [correct] Known accessibility issues
    2. [correct] Website accessibility features
    3. [correct] Statement of commitment
    4. [correct] Statement of compliance
    5. [incorrect] The name of the website's developer

Back to Self-Test 6

Self-Test 7

1. When vendors are describing the level of accessibility their product complies with, they should mention Level AAA.
    1. [incorrect] True
    2. [correct] False
2. If a vendor mentions a few known accessibility issues in their accessibility statement for a product, purchasing or licensing the product should be avoided.
    1. [incorrect] True
    2. [correct] False

Back to Self-Test 7

Self-Test 8

1. When hiring a new graduate web developer, they should list at least one course they took on web accessibility.

    1. [incorrect] True
    2. [correct] False
2. Workplace accommodations for a person who is blind would typically include which of the following technologies? Choose all that apply.
    1. [correct] Screen reader
    2. [incorrect] Voice recognition
    3. [incorrect] Trackball
    4. [incorrect] Text-to-speech
    5. [incorrect] Screen magnification

Back to Self-Test 8

Self-Test 9

1. Described in Accessibility Awareness Requirements in Other Organizational Roles, it is important for management to have the following accessibility-related knowledge. Choose all that apply.
    1. [correct] Knowledge of local and relevant international accessibility-related regulations
    2. [correct] Knowledge of accessibility policy
    3. [incorrect] Knowledge of disabilities and associated barriers
    4. [incorrect] Document accessibility (e.g., invoices, receipts, and product specifications)
    5. [incorrect] User interface accessibility design
2. Which of the following would be a typical accommodation for a person with fine-motor impairment? Choose all that apply.
    1. [correct] Speech recognition software
    2. [correct] Eye tracking hardware
    3. [correct] Button switch hardware
    4. [correct] Large-key keyboard
    5. [incorrect] Screen reader software
    6. [incorrect] Screen magnification software
    7. [correct] Head mouse hardware

Back to Self-Test 9

Answer Key: Final Project

Sharp Clothing Company Digital Accessibility Policy

Effective Date: July 7, 2017

Background

Why is a digital accessibility policy necessary?

The Sharp Clothing Company (the company), being based in Ontario, Canada, is required under the *Accessibility for Ontarians with Disabilities Act* (AODA 2005), to ensure its digital information is accessible to people with disabilities.

Commitment

The Company is committed to improving and maintaining access to its digital information. First, as a social responsibility, to ensure no one is excluded from working at, or being a customer of, the company. Second, in its efforts to expand its market coverage, the company will ensure its accessibility standards meet those for an international audience.

Accessibility Committee

The Accessibility Committee (AC) will be made up of senior representatives and knowledgeable staff from each of the company's departments. The committee will meet quarterly and when necessary to address significant accessibility-related issues

The AC will be led by the accessibility coordinator (i.e., the Accessibility Champion).

SCOPE AND GOALS

The AC will be responsible for:

- Raising accessibility awareness
- Encouraging feedback to share problems and solutions
- Implementing quality-assurance procedures
- Handling legal matters related to accessibility
- Providing web and digital accessibility support
- Developing internal accessibility standards
- Representing the organization in public affairs related to accessibility

AUTHORITY AND ENFORCEMENT

The AC will have the authority to make adjustments to current processes throughout the company to ensure that accessibility requirements are being met.

The AC will also have the authority to delay release of products to the public, if accessibility does not meet company accessibility standards.

The AC will have the authority to recommend dismissal of staff who are unwilling to follow or repeatedly disregard the company's accessibility standards or policies.

SUPPORT

The accessibility coordinator will be the main point of contact for company staff who have questions or concerns related to digital accessibility.

The accessibility coordinator will be the main point of contact for the public with digital accessibility-related enquiries.

The AC will maintain a digital accessibility knowledge base within the company's main website, which will be available for all staff.

In the Contact Us form on the company website, "accessibility" will be included as a reason for the contact among the other given options. When selected, enquiries will be sent directly to the accessibility coordinator. The accessibility coordinator will direct the enquiry to the appropriate person (if required) as soon as it is feasible to do so, or will respond as soon as possible, taking no longer than 24 hours to reply.

Guidelines and Standards

The AC will be responsible for developing and maintaining a set of company digital accessibility guidelines. These guidelines will include:

- Website and Web Application Accessibility Guidelines
- Web Content Accessibility Guidelines
- Document Accessibility Guidelines
- Multimedia Accessibility Guidelines

WEBSITE DEVELOPMENT

The company websites, or any website or application created after this policy is issued, shall meet WCAG Level AA requirements outlined in the company's Website and Web Application Accessibility Guidelines, except where it is unrealistic to do so or where undue hardship has been established.

Undue hardship will be determined by the AC in cases where the cost is excessive, where technology or an equivalent does not exist in an accessible form, where health or safety are at risk, and where external funding is unavailable to assist with excessive costs.

WEBSITE CONTENT

All content added to the website after this policy is issued shall meet WCAG Level AA requirements outlined in the company's Web Content Accessibility Guidelines.

DOCUMENTS AND COMMUNICATIONS

All documents and communications authored after this policy is issued will meet the requirements of the company's Document Accessibility Guidelines.

MULTIMEDIA

All multimedia produced by the company after this policy is issued will have captions for video and transcripts for audio, as outlined in the company's Multimedia Accessibility Guidelines.

THIRD-PARTY DIGITAL CONTENT

Where third-party documents, web content, or web applications are used after all effort has been made to obtain these in an accessible form, the company will not be responsible for their lack of accessibility, and the company will acknowledge this fact in a way that is accessible and easily discoverable by customers or employees.

Hiring Equity and Employment Accommodation

The company will make an effort to hire qualified people with disabilities, and where candidate qualifications are comparable, favour the person with a disability.

The company will question candidates about digital accessibility related to the position for which the candidate is applying; and where candidates are comparable, the company will favour those with more accessibility knowledge.

The company will provide appropriate assistive technology or other accommodation for any employee making such a request and can demonstrate an associated disability.

The company will establish and maintain a full-time Accessibility Specialist position and, within one year of this policy being established, hire a person with digital accessibility expertise for the role of accessibility coordinator or to act as a consultant, taking on the role of Accessibility Engineer within the company's IT group.

Training and Awareness

The AC will develop and maintain a series of educational units on various aspects of digital accessibility, consisting of documents, videos, web-based training, and in-class workshops, that will be offered periodically to ensure staff are adequately trained on accessibility issues associated with their position. These units will include:

- Accessible Document Authoring
- How People with Disabilities Use the Web
- Basic Web Accessibility
- Advanced Web Accessibility with WAI-ARIA

- Web Accessibility Auditing
- Multimedia Captioning

The AC will also be responsible for creating and maintaining an accessibility statement to be linked prominently on the main website. The statement will describe the company's commitment to accessibility and outlines accessibility features available on the website to assist users navigating the site with assistive technology.

Digital Accessibility Resources

The AC will establish and maintain the company's accessibility knowledge base, which will contain a variety of resources including:

- The company accessibility guidelines
- Documentation on web and document accessibility methods
- Instructional videos on digital accessibility
- Annual accessibility reports
- Templates for Requests for Proposals (RFP) and contract accessibility wording
- Promotional items to highlight company accessibility efforts

Procurement

All Requests for Proposals (RFP) involving digital content or products will include wording that requests details regarding a product's accessibility. Accessibility will be prioritized when judging proposals, so that lack of accessibility is likely to disqualify or significantly disadvantage a vendor.

Contracts with vendors will include language that commits the vendor to supplying products at an agreed-upon level of accessibility. Vendors will be obligated to address accessibility issues not previously acknowledged and/or dismissed.

Purchasing will acquire products and service that are the most accessible, except in cases where there is not a satisfactory or comparable product with a given set of features or functionality that provides accessibility.

The AC will prepare templates for RFP and contract language and maintain them through the company's accessibility knowledge base.

Accessibility Auditing and Quality Assurance

Accessibility quality assurance will be added to and maintained throughout the company's processes. Before digital content is distributed publicly, it must be reviewed by someone other than the author who is familiar with the accessibility elements that the type of content being reviewed entails. This will include all documents, content posted to the websites, and promotional materials distributed to the public.

In the case of website development, the author's code will be reviewed by another knowledgeable IT staff member; and before the development is made available to the public, it will be reviewed by the accessibility coordinator. Where the accessibility coordinator identifies issues, those issues must be corrected on the recommendation of the accessibility coordinator.

Monitoring and Periodic Reviews

The accessibility coordinator will be responsible for conducting periodic spot checks on digital content and for conducting annual accessibility audits on the company's websites.

Any issues identified during checks and audits will be directed to those responsible for the content in question, who will be required to address the issues as instructed by the accessibility coordinator.

In cases where checks fail consistently, the accessibility coordinator will arrange additional training for the employee(s) responsible for the failures.

Reporting

Following the annual audit of the company's websites, the accessibility coordinator, with the assistance of the AC, will produce a formal report on the accessibility status of the company's websites. The status report will be presented at the next quarterly senior management meeting and archived in the accessibility knowledge base.

Policy Review

This policy will be reviewed annually by the AC and adjustments made where necessary. If modified, the policy will be approved by the company's senior director within 30 days of the update.

Index